How's It Going?

How's It Going?
A Practical Guide to Conferring With Student Writers

Carl Anderson

Heinemann
Portsmouth, NH

KH

Heinemann
A division of Reed Elsevier Inc.
361 Hanover Street
Portsmouth, NH 03801-3912
Offices and agents throughout the world

www.heinemann.com

The author and publisher wish to thank those who granted permission to reprint borrowed material:

Excerpt from "So a Big, Bad Bully is Coming After You" by Candace Purdom. Originally published in the Chicago Tribune, August 20, 1994. Reprinted by permission of the author.

Excerpt from "The Police Bullies" by Bob Herbert. Copyright © 1997 by the New York Times Co. Reprinted by permission.

"Spring Is" by Bobbi Katz. Copyright © 1979 by Bobbi Katz. Used by permission of the author.

Library of Congress Cataloging-in-Publication Data
Anderson, Carl, educator.
    How's it going? : a practical guide to conferring with student writers / Carl Anderson.
        p.   cm
    Includes bibliographical references (p.) and index.
    ISBN 0-325-00224-X (alk. paper)
    1. English language—Composition and exercises—Study and teaching (Elementary) 2. Creative writing—Study and teaching (Elementary) I. Title.

LB1576 .A6159 2000
372.62′3044—dc21

00-035059

Editor: Bill Varner
Production: Renee Nicholls
Front cover photograph: Donnelly Marks
Back cover photograph: Roy Silverstein
Cover design: Catherine Hawkes/Cat & Mouse
Manufacturing: Louise Richardson

Printed in the United States of America on acid-free paper
08 07 06 05   RRD   13 14 15

12/13/05

For Robin
who always confers with love

Contents

Acknowledgments

I want to give my first thanks to Lucy Calkins. In the winter of 1988, I was in my second year of teaching and was trying to decide whether to switch careers. Then I heard Lucy speak about teaching writing at one of the Teachers College Reading and Writing Project's Saturday conferences. Lucy's words, filled with her passion for teaching and deep admiration for children, inspired me right then and there to make teaching my life's work. In the years since that Saturday, Lucy has been one of my life's greatest teachers. And since I joined the Project in 1994, she has been my mentor and friend. Her belief in me enabled me to write this book, and her wise suggestions helped me write it well.

It has been a privilege and a joy to work as a staff developer for the Project. Several of my colleagues have made especially important contributions to my thinking and writing. Randy Bomer, then co-director of the Project, was the first person I told I wanted to write a book on conferring. His enthusiastic response to the idea and to my first two chapters gave me the confidence I needed to stay with the project. Isoke Nia, Donna Santman, and Kathleen Tolan shared their thinking about rigorous workshop teaching with the Project community, helping me improve my conferring, and thus this book, too. Indeed, I got the idea for this book while showing teachers a videotape of Kathleen Tolan's brilliant conferences at P.S. 125 in Harlem. My rich friendships with Sharon Hill and Teresa Caccavale, developed on long plane rides to and from Missouri and Kentucky where we worked together in schools, sustained me as I wrote. Both of them listened to me talk about the ups and downs of writing a book, and gave me support and encouragement whenever I needed it.

I am grateful to everyone who has attended the Project's Thursday think tanks. Much of our thinking together about literacy teaching is reflected in the pages of this book. In addition to the colleagues mentioned above, I want to thank Pam Allyn, Janet Angelillo, Mimi Aronson, Katherine Bomer, Lydia Bellino, Peter Brunn, Grace Chough, Mina Chudasama, Mary Ann Colbert, Kathy Collins, Kathy Doyle, Kristen Eagleburger, Lynne Einbender, Nick Flynn, Antoinette Fornshell, Jane Fraser, Rory Freed, Jacqui Getz, Elise Goldman, Lynn Holcomb, Holly Kim, Gaby Layden, Bonnie Leitstein, Amy Ludwig, Shirley McPhillips, Derek Miller, Kate Montgomery, Priscilla Moody, Deena Nusblatt, Laurie Pessah, Liz Phillips, Susan Radley, Anna Reduce, Lisa Ripperger, Kim Tarpinian, Dolores Totillo, Patty Vitale, Artie Voigt, and Edie Ziegler. I am also grateful for the ongoing contributions that Joanne Hindley and Katie Wood Ray make to the Project community.

I want to thank Maury Brooks, Michelle Bugay, Susan Forrest, Marla Julien, Betsey McGee, Denise Montalbano, Beth Neville, Lace Robinson, and Laurie Roddy, who were members of the Project's central office staff during the time I wrote the book. By helping the Project run so smoothly, they made my life run more smoothly.

I am grateful for my time spent with teachers and administrators in schools in New York City, its surrounding suburbs, and around the country. I am especially thankful that teachers in many schools were interested in studying conferring with me: P.S. 6, in New York City's District 2; M.S. 54, in District 3; P.S. 155, in District 4; M.S. 45, in District 10; P.S. 261, P.S. 321, and M.S. 51, in District 15; Birch School, Chatterton School, and Lakeside School, in Merrick, Long Island; Indian Hills School, in Holmdel, New Jersey; Goshen Elementary School, in Goshen, Kentucky; and Derby Ridge Elementary School, in Columbia, Missouri. I want to thank Project Construct and the Missouri Department of Elementary and Secondary Education for making my work possible at Derby Ridge Elementary School.

Generous funding of the Project's Leadership Development Project by the J.P. Morgan Charitable Trust, the Booth Ferris Foundation, and Joseph Seagram & Sons, Inc., allowed me to lead a group of teachers and staff developers in a yearlong study of conferring during the 1997–98 school year. What a gift it was for me to study with Peter Brunn, Mina Chudasama, Dana Hill, Mark Hardy, Holly Kim, Barbara Rosenblum, Alexa Stott, and Dolores Totillo that year. The thinking we did together shapes the entire book.

Of course, the students I have conferred with have been my most important teachers. I wish I could personally thank each of the students I taught at Holy Spirit School in the Bronx; Bardstown Middle School in Bardstown, Kentucky; and Wood Oaks Junior High School in Northbrook, Illinois; as well as the students I have worked with during my time at the Project. I want to give special thanks to the students who appear in the pages of this book.

With a generous gift from Jeanne and Jeffrey Levy-Hinte, the Project purchased laptop computers. I couldn't have written this book without one of the laptops.

Numerous people have read and responded to the manuscript at various stages of its development. Pam Allyn, Janet Angelillo, Randy Bomer, Lucy Calkins, Teresa Caccavale, Robin Epstein, Jane Fraser, Sharon Hill, Shirley McPhillips, Laurie Pessah, and Susan Pliner read early drafts. Lucy, Laurie, Robin, Kate Montgomery, and Brenda Wallace read the entire manuscript. The book is a much better one than it would have been without their feedback.

I want to thank Lynn Herschlein and Don Murray for their enthusiastic readings of the manuscript, as well as their insightful comments. Their reactions gave me the energy I needed to go the distance and make my final series of revisions.

I am grateful for the guidance given to me by my editors at Heinemann. I appreciated the excitement with which Scott Mahler responded to my initial proposal. During the writing of the manuscript, Bill Varner conferred with me wisely at all the important junctures. I am glad that Bill became a new father in the middle of this project so that he could better appreciate what it was like for me to be a new father and write a book at the same time. And I am grateful for Renée Nicholls's meticulous copyediting, as well as the care she and Renee Le Verrier gave the book as it moved through each stage of production.

I am indebted to Wanda Troy for conferring with me about the book's title.

I want to thank several of my own teachers for their support and guidance. My eighth-grade English teacher, Maryann Costa, told me twenty-five years ago that I would someday write a book. What an impact those words had on my life. I'll never forget the thoughtful responses Syd Nathans and Peter Wood gave to my writing when I was an undergraduate at Duke University. And I'll never forget that my instructors and professors at the University of Louisville's School of Education—Jean Hicks, Ric Hovda, Marjorie Kaiser, and Lea Smith—believed that I would grow into a fine teacher.

I am thankful for the conversations about literacy teaching that I had with colleagues during my days when I was a classroom teacher: Brian McCarthy, at Holy Spirit School; Chris Luvisi, at Bardstown Middle School; and Mary Lou Gilliam and Carol Rennolds, at Wood Oaks Junior High School.

I am grateful for the friendship of Artie and Paula Voigt. They made sure that I didn't take writing a book too seriously, and the laughter we shared in their Point Lookout home always helped me return to my writing reenergized.

As always, I appreciate the love and support of my parents, Helen and Kenneth Anderson. This book has its deepest roots in the love that they, both educators themselves, had for the students they taught. I am also grateful for the love and support of my in-laws, Harold and Marcia Epstein, and the encouragement they have given me since the first day I began working on the book.

I give my final—and most heartfelt—thanks to Robin Epstein, to whom this book is dedicated. I am thankful, of course, for the remarkable patience she had for my late-night and weekend-morning writing sessions. I am more thankful, however, for the impatience I sensed underneath her cheerful "Good luck with your writing" every time I left our apartment with my laptop to go write in a local coffeeshop. Robin and I share a wonderful life with our daughter, Anzia. Knowing that Robin and Anzia were hoping I would soon rejoin them kept me focused and productive. For that reason it was a joy each day to be finished writing. And for that reason it is a joy—finally—to be finished with the book.

Foreword

My oldest son, Miles, loves to read big fantasy novels, in which the characters search long and hard and finally, at the end of the long road, are given a manual for magic. You and I have also searched long and hard for magic. We've known for a long time that while there are no guideposts for the other aspects of teaching writing, at the entrance to the land of writing conferences, there's a sign that says, "Herein lie the dragons." When it comes to conferring—the central act of teaching writing—there has been no place to turn for an illuminating map—until now. Carl Anderson's *How's It Going?: A Practical Guide to Conferring With Student Writers* leads us through the challenging but essential terrain of learning to confer with unflinching honesty and clarity.

Once we've learned how to confer well, we've got a power chip that never quits. It generates original, strong teaching each day, each year, for every writer, forever and ever. When we learn about the teaching of writing, conferring is the subject that promises the biggest payoff, for it is the foundation of writing workshop.

In *How's It Going?*, Carl names the components of conferences, giving teachers a way to plot their course through these often fleeting conversations. How reassuring it is to see that the hundreds of conferences we hold each year are all variations of a few themes. How helpful it is to enter conferences knowing we'll face several key decision points, junctions that offer us a predictable set of options.

For years now, teachers connected to the Teachers College Reading and Writing Project community have moved heaven and earth in order to have Carl by their side, demonstrating, watching, and coaching them as they grow stronger at conferring and as teachers of writing. I find Carl to be the consummate teacher. He does not overwhelm, dazzle, or distract us with needless displays of his prowess. His goal is not for us to become convinced he is smart and capable, but rather it is for us to realize we are smart and capable. At the Project, he is our Lead Staff Developer, responsible not only for designing and conducting literacy professional development in schools—which under his tutelage are becoming mentor schools for all of New York City—but also for coaching and counseling newer Project staff members. I sometimes joke that sending teachers who have recently joined our staff out in the field to apprentice with Carl is like sprinkling Miracle-Gro on them. Their mini-lessons become more efficient, their conferences more rigorous, and their thinking about curriculum more principled. Carl scaffolds and guides in ways that make all of us—his students and colleagues alike—metamorphose into more than we dreamt we could be. Now Carl brings this gift to his readers.

As we travel through the pages of the book, Carl is with us every step of the way. One of the extraordinary things about *How's It Going?* is that it not only describes effective conferences, it teaches us how to lead them. It's as if Carl pulls up a chair beside us, his readers, notices what we are already doing, and shows us new possibilities in our teaching. He steers us around traps and pitfalls and kindly nudges us to "have a go." Together with Carl, we find the answers to common questions such as, "What can I say that'll actually help my students become better writers?" and "What do I do if their pieces look fine to me?" and "How do I respond when students say they're finished and have no intention of revising?" Chapters explore all the major issues of conferring, from the role of the teacher and student in a writing conference, to using writing mentors, to classroom management. All the way through the book, we're led toward becoming more skilled, planful, and efficient teachers of writing.

Carl began his teaching life at age sixteen as a sailing instructor on Long Island's Great South Bay. He taught sailing for twelve years, helping children become champion racers and imparting to them a lifelong love of the wind and water. Often now, when he finishes a keynote address, someone from the audience will approach him and say, "Do you remember me? You taught my son to sail. He still talks about you." Dedication and passion have always been the hallmarks of Carl Anderson's teaching. I am so glad that with the publication of *How's It Going?*, every writing teacher in the world can now benefit from Carl's close-in coaching and become strong and clear about conferring, the central act of their teaching. For our writing workshops will come alive only if we tame the dragons and learn to confer well. It is my great pleasure to invite you to join Carl in these pages and discover how to master the magic of conferring.

—Lucy Calkins

Introduction

During the months before our daughter, Anzia, was born, my wife, Robin, worked hard to prepare herself for the birth and the challenges that would lay beyond. I, on the other hand, worked myself into a state of panic.

One evening, I called my friend Artie Voigt. Before he could finish saying "Hey, buddy," I started babbling.

"What's your opinion of wipe warmers? There's this one model that's called "Waldo the Wipe Warmer"—it's this electric penguin that wraps around the box of wipes. You know, if I were a baby, I wouldn't want my butt to be cleaned with a freezing cold wipe, especially in the middle of the night. Do you think we should get one?"

Artie was chuckling, but I hardly heard him.

"Another thing," I continued. "Diapers. Most of them seem to fasten with tape. That's fine, but what if I peel off the tape to check if the diaper is dirty, and it's not? I've ruined the diaper. But there's this more expensive brand that uses Velcro instead. You can fasten and unfasten these diapers as many times as you like. We can't decide which kind we should use."

Artie was still chuckling.

"And there are five models of strollers we're considering. Can I tell you about each one and see what you think?"

There was nothing but silence on the other end of the phone. When Artie was silent, I knew he was about to be serious.

1

"Waldo the Wipe Warmer?" Artie began. "We didn't even have *Where's Waldo?* books when my girls were babies. I changed lots of diapers, but whether they were fastened with tape or Velcro—or Crazy Glue—I don't remember. And if a stroller has four wheels, it's a good stroller."

Artie wasn't helping at all. I saw an image in my mind of two hospital rooms, one in the birthing center where my wife was cradling our newborn baby in her arms, the other in the psychiatric ward where I was in a straitjacket.

"But none of this matters," Artie continued. "What really matters is this. You've got to keep the baby in a clean diaper and in dry clothes, start there. Feed her when she's hungry. Hold her when she cries. Read her lots of books. And the most important thing is love her until it hurts. Then love her even more."

I became a father not long after my phone conversation with Artie. A few hours after Anzia was born, I changed my first diaper—whether it fastened with tape or with Velcro, I don't recall. My wife and I received a Waldo the Wipe Warmer as a gift, but our daughter never seemed to care whether wipes were hot or cold. And my wife still regrets that we didn't get the red plaid stroller, instead of the blue plaid one.

But I soon found out that Artie was right about what really mattered. Keeping Anzia clean, fed, comforted, read to, and, above all, loved—these were the essentials of parenting our baby daughter.

As Lead Staff Developer for the Teachers College Reading and Writing Project, led by founding director Lucy Calkins, I have the privilege of working side by side with teachers in New York City and across the country in their writing workshops. In order to help teachers excel at the teaching of writing, I draw on my years of experience as an elementary and middle school teacher and on insights generated by the many creative and collegial educators in the Reading and Writing Project's literacy think tank.

I spend much of my time in classrooms helping teachers with writing conferences, the one-on-one conversations about students' writing that are the heart of workshop teaching. As soon as we start talking about conferring, teachers pepper me with questions: What should I say to start my conferences? What should I do when a student says he's finished and has no intention of revising? How long should conferences be? What record-keeping form works best? And so on.

Because I want teachers to know I understand why they have so many questions, I often tell the story of my pre-fatherhood anxiety attack. Conferring, after all, often creates a feeling of anxiety—even panic—in us, whether we are new to workshop teaching or we are workshop veterans. Just like parenting is one of our most important responsibilities, conferring with students is our most crucial writing workshop role. We launch writing workshops in our classrooms because the writing workshop is a structure that allows us to teach students individually in conferences, even in classrooms that contain thirty or forty students. Writing conferences aren't the icing on the cake; they *are* the cake.

Teachers have told me they have doubts that they can learn to confer well, their misgivings sometimes growing deeper after they watch me do it. "There's no way I'll be able to do what you just did in those conferences," they say. When I press them to explain, they reply, "You have such an easy way with kids," or "You know so much about writing." I know these comments have an unspoken subtext: *I won't be able to confer because I'm not as comfortable talking with students one on one; I won't have anything to say to students because I don't have his writing experience.*

In my early days as a staff developer I was puzzled about how to respond to such comments. I realized eventually that many teachers doubted themselves because they couldn't see past me when I conferred with students. That is, they zeroed in on aspects of my conferring that had to do with who I am—such as my way of relating to children and my personal knowledge of writing—that they couldn't duplicate.

Who we are and what our experiences have been are factors that come into play in writing conferences, factors that by definition differ from teacher to teacher. Our personalities—gregarious or taciturn, friendly or reserved—influence our conferences, as do our choices about whether to relate to students in a casual or formal manner.

But there isn't one personality trait correct for conferring, nor is there a required kind of writing experience. All kinds of teachers with all kinds of writing experiences can make conferring their own and can confer well. Just like with parenting, when we keep certain conferring essentials in mind, we can confer well every day in our writing workshops. These essentials are the subject of this book.

This book grew out of a four-year study. During this time, I've studied how to help teachers new to writing workshop learn to confer and how to help experienced workshop teachers improve their conferring practice. The study has had three parts.

First, I began by rereading the thoughtful chapters written about conferring in books authored by Donald Murray (1985), Donald Graves (1983), Lucy Calkins (1994), Nancie Atwell (1998), Georgia

Heard (1989), Shelley Harwayne (1992), Tom Romano (1987), Joanne Hindley (1996), and others. As I read, I tried to look past the aspects of their conferences that most reflect who these authors are as individuals, and instead focused on the aspects the teachers I work with could learn to do.

Second, I analyzed my own conferences, as well as those of my colleagues at the Project and those of the gifted teachers of writing that are part of the Project community.

Third, I studied conferring with hundreds of teachers in schools in New York City and its surrounding suburbs, and in districts all across the United States. As I worked with these teachers in their classrooms, and spoke to them in workshops and at institutes at Teachers College, I stood on the shoulders of all who have thought and written about conferring before me. At first, I used the words of others to describe effective conferences. But as my study continued, I created my own language and ways of thinking about conferring.

As I wrote this book, I imagined myself working as a staff developer alongside you, the reader, in your classroom. I imagined you as a classroom teacher, or as a student preparing to be a teacher, and that you have an ongoing writing workshop in your classroom, or you soon will. You probably begin your workshop each day by giving a mini-lesson—a short whole-class lesson—and then, as your students work on their writing for the next half hour, you meet individually with four or five students in conferences that last about five minutes each. You end the workshop by bringing your students together again for a brief share session.

Throughout the book, whenever I describe conferences with students, I imagined you were at my side as I conferred. And I've filled the book with the kind of practical advice and descriptions of conferring techniques I offer teachers in the course of my work with them—the same advice I would offer you if I were working in your classroom.

I've also imagined how you might use this book. You might, for example, tape-record some of your conferences or type out transcripts of conferences to analyze as you read. You might read the book with a colleague or in a study group, and visit each other's classrooms to watch conferences, and discuss them afterwards. Or you might visit with those same colleagues' classrooms and confer with students together, stopping at important junctures in the conferences to discuss what each of you is thinking and what you might do next.

Finally, I've imagined that you are doing other kinds of work to help you improve your conferring. You make time to write yourself.

You read about other writers and pay particular attention to learning about their individual writing processes. You read across many different genres—memoir, poetry, short fiction, editorials, feature articles, and so forth—and as you read, you try to think about what makes each piece a quality piece of writing. You read books on writing. And you learn as much as you can about the writers in your classrooms. What you learn from doing these kinds of work will give you knowledge you'll need to confer well.

Chapter 1 is a discussion of the essential concepts of conferring. In Chapters 2 and 3, I consider our conference role and how to teach students to fulfill theirs. Chapter 4 is about using literature as we confer. In Chapter 5, I discuss the impact that mini-lessons have on conferences. Chapter 6 contains thoughts about the planning we need to do before we confer. And in Chapter 7, I suggest class management techniques that make it possible for us to confer.

This book will not make conferring easy. There is no script that guarantees a magnificent conference. After fourteen years as a teacher and staff developer, I still find each writing conference with a student to be a unique—and sometimes difficult—challenge. We can, however, learn ways of thinking, develop repertoires of techniques, and perfect straightforward strategies that will boost our conferring power. That's the goal of this book—to help teachers grasp the art and logic of conferring, and with this learning in mind, to confer well.

References

Atwell, Nancie. 1998. *In the Middle.* Portsmouth, NH: Heinemann.

Calkins, Lucy. 1994. *The Art of Teaching Writing.* Portsmouth, NH: Heinemann.

Graves, Donald. 1983. *Writing: Teachers & Children at Work.* Portsmouth, NH: Heinemann.

Harwayne, Shelley. 1992. *Lasting Impressions.* Portsmouth, NH: Heinemann.

Heard, Georgia. 1989. *For the Good of the Earth and Sun.* Portsmouth, NH. Heinemann.

Hindley, Joanne. 1996. *In the Company of Children.* York, ME: Stenhouse.

Murray, Donald M. 1985. *A Writer Teaches Writing.* Boston: Houghton Mifflin.

Romano, Tom. 1987. *Clearing the Way.* Portsmouth, NH: Heinemann.

1 Conferences Are Conversations

At the end of my first year of teaching, I felt I had failed. I had gone into teaching because I'd imagined I would enjoy the relationships with students. But I spent almost all of that first year standing in the front of my classroom, talking *at* my sixth graders, not *with* them. Consequently, I didn't know any of them well. Some were just a name on the roll. For a time, I seriously considered pursuing a doctorate in history. I figured that my relationships with the dead people I would be writing about as a historian would be more vital than those I had with the students who sat in my classroom for one hundred and eighty days.

I changed my mind about history graduate school after a friend gave me a copy of Lucy Calkins' *The Art of Teaching Writing* (First Edition, 1986). Like many other teachers, I was immediately struck by the pieces of student writing Calkins included in the book. It was a revelation to me that students could have so much to say about their lives in their writing.

But it was an even bigger revelation to me that in the writing workshops Calkins described, teachers and students had so much to say to each other. It was the teacher's role during every workshop period, in fact, to initiate conversations with students about the pieces they were writing.

It was the promise of these teacher-student conversations—which Calkins called writing conferences—that convinced me to launch a writing workshop in my classroom the next year. I imagined—correctly, as it turned out—that these conversations would give me the means to really get to know students, and to have relationships with them that mattered.

Although today I see conferences as a means to get to know students *and* as a powerful way of teaching them to be better writers, I have never stopped considering these one-on-one talks as conversations. When I talk about them publicly, I call them writing conferences, simply because that's what my colleagues at the Teachers College Reading and Writing Project and across the country call them. But inside, I've held onto the word *conversation* because the word suggests so many things about the way I believe we should talk with students about their writing.

If you make a picture in your mind of a conversation you've had with someone you care about, you probably see a colleague, a friend, a relative. Connected to that person you probably see a certain kind of place—a table in a restaurant, a path in the woods, the stoop of your apartment building. And you probably hear a certain kind of talk—it's intimate, personal, shared. This is the kind feeling I want to create as I talk with students about their writing.

I also use the word *conversation* because even though in a conference we are teachers talking with students, we are also writers talking to writers. In *A Writer Teaches Writing*, Don Murray (1985) explains that the act of writing we have in common with students puts us on a level with them and them on a level with us:

> [Conferences] are not mini-lectures but the working talk of fellow writers sharing their experience with the writing process. At times, of course, they will be teacher and student, master and apprentice, if you want, but most of the time they will be remarkably close to peers, because each writer, no matter how experienced, begins again with each draft. (148)

There are other implications to using the word *conversation* to describe conferences besides suggesting the tone of our interactions with students and our relationship to them. Conferences, like many conversations, have the following characteristics:

- Conferences have a point to them.
- Conferences have a predictable structure.
- In conferences, we pursue lines of thinking with students.
- Teachers and students have conversational roles in conferences.
- In conferences, we show students we care about them.

In the following sections, I discuss each of these characteristics of conferences.

Conferences Are Focused on Helping Students Become Better Writers

When I talk about conferences as conversations, many teachers ask me, "What are these conversations *about*?"

I tell these teachers they've asked a crucial question about conferring, if not *the* crucial question. After all, we expect that many conversations will have a point to them. When these conversations don't meet this expectation, we feel confused and frustrated. We say, "That conversation didn't go anywhere," or "That talk was all over the place." Our conferences go well only if we—and our students—know why we're having the conversations.

The point of the writing conference conversation, then, is this: we confer with students to help them become better writers. By "better writers" I mean writers who can do the work we teach them in today's conferences on their own in future pieces. In *The Art of Teaching Writing*, Lucy Calkins (1994) explains that our challenge in conferences is to stay focused on the students with whom we're conferring and their growth as writers:

> If we can keep only one thing in mind—and I fail at this half the time—it is that we are teaching the writer and not the writing. Our decisions must be guided by "what might help this *writer*" rather than "what might help this *writing*." If the piece of writing gets better but the writer has learned nothing that will help him or her another day on another piece, then the conference was a waste of everyone's time. It may even have done more harm than good, for such conferences teach students not to trust their own reactions. (228)

This is not as obvious as it sounds. I've watched many well-intentioned teachers get sidetracked during conferences and lose sight of why they're conferring.

Some teachers, for example, get mesmerized by what their students are writing *about*. They end up having a long conversation with Demeka about her salamander or with Daniel about the summer he spent in Alabama, conversations that do little to help children grow as writers.

Sometimes these conversations about the content of students' pieces turn into therapy sessions. While writing about their lives is therapeutic for some students, we need to remember that we are writing teachers, not therapists. If we are worried about certain children, we should refer them to the school psychologist or guidance counselor.

Other teachers can't resist the urge to fix up everything that may be wrong with their students' drafts. They find it hard to bite their tongues when they can come up with the perfect lead for a student's piece. Or they fear that if the student's piece still contains weaknesses when it's published, they will be judged by parents, colleagues, and principals to be poor teachers.

If we take control over a student's writing and make sure that the draft has our perfect lead or our brilliant dialogue, all we've done is given a demonstration of our expertise as writers. We shouldn't confuse this with helping students develop their own expertise. A teacher fixing up students' drafts no more helps them grow than a coach standing in for players in a basketball game helps those players improve.

One way we help students become better writers is by teaching them strategies and techniques more experienced writers use to write well. When we finish a conference, we hope we can say to ourselves, "I taught Erika a strategy for spelling an unfamiliar word," or "I taught Jemel how he could use short sentences to create emphasis." By having students try what we teach them in the piece of writing they're currently working on, we give them the opportunity to learn what we've taught so they can use the strategy or technique *for the rest of their writing lives.*

In other conferences, we help students become better writers by teaching them to teach themselves. That is, we nudge students to figure out what strategies or techniques will help them do what they want to do as writers, or how they can better use the strategies or techniques they're already using. At the end of these conferences, we want to be able to say, "I helped Angela realize she could tape another piece of paper to her draft so she could add on to her story," or "I helped Jemel figure out there are other ways he can write narratives than starting when he woke up and ending when he went to bed." When conferences are times when students teach themselves, they not only learn about strategies and techniques they can use the rest of their writing lives, but they also learn about being writers who can teach themselves at any time while they're writing.

Another way we help students become better writers is by teaching them to be reflective about their writing. There's more to writing well, after all, than having repertoires of strategies and techniques. Good writers use strategies and techniques *thoughtfully* because they've learned to step back from their writing and reflect on what they're doing. They ask themselves questions such as "How's this going?" and "What am I trying to do here?" and "What do I need to do to make this work?" When we ask students, "How's it going?" or "What work are you doing as a writer today?" or "What can I help you with today?" we are scaffolding their growth into reflective writers. When we ask these same questions in conference after conference, students begin to ask these questions themselves—independent of us.

When we finish a conference, we should be able to name what it is we did to help that student become a better writer. Let's give this naming a try. We'll look at a transcript of a conference I had with Doran, a student in Lisa Emond's fifth-grade class in P.S. 261 in Brooklyn. Doran wanted to write a feature article on how parents and kids could get the best prices on toys. He had spent the previous week writing entries in his writers notebook about some of the different strategies he knew for beating high prices. He had also studied several feature articles, such as one written by journalist Candace Purdom (1994) entitled "So a big, bad bully is coming after you . . ."

CARL: How's it going?

DORAN: Well, I'm working on my article.

CARL: Working on my article?

DORAN: Well, okay, I'm just getting started.

CARL: So does that mean you're ready to start writing your lead?

DORAN: Yeah.

CARL: Could you tell me why you think you're ready to start your lead?

DORAN: Well, I made a list of my bullets [subsections]. [See Figure 1–1.]

CARL: So you made a plan for the article?

DORAN: Yeah. At first I was just listing the parts, but then I thought a little bit like which would go one after the other, to make sense. So I did a part about Toys 'R' Us, then I did one about the difference between stores, and then I have here waiting toys out, and buying toys quick, and then I have coupons over here. I tried to match them near another one so it would kind of make sense.

CARL: So you're trying to group the parts together.

DORAN: Right.

CARL: So your subject is toys, and your angle is getting the best deal on toys?

DORAN: Right.

CARL: So this article will help people get that deal. You know, I can't believe how much toys cost, even for babies, so you're doing people like me—parents—a real service here.

DORAN: Uh-huh.

CARL: So how are you going to get started with your draft?

DORAN: Well, I guess first I'm just going to think about my lead and write about what my angle is, like at the beginning of the bully article [see Figure 1–2] . . . it's telling about what the angle is and everything. So I guess I'd start by thinking about my lead and doing that . . . and once that was done, I'd look back on these entries [in his writers notebook] and make them bigger and add things on . . . and we're planning to go to maybe a toy store or

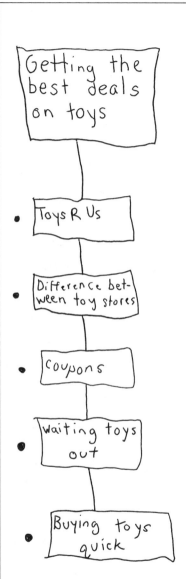

FIGURE 1–1   Doran's plan for his feature article

Bigger than Shaquille. Meaner than the Wicked Witch of the West. Scarier than a raptor. We're talking about the school bully.

"Bullies are angry little kids," says psychologist Alan Hirsch of the Chicago area's Capable Kid Counseling Centers. "I've worked with kids who are proud that they're bullying other children."

Often they feel bad about themselves, so bullies take it out on others. Yeah, we know, it's hard to feel sorry for someone who makes your life miserable. Here are tips on making a tough spot easier:

FIGURE 1–2   Lead of Candace Purdom's, "So a big, bad bully is coming after you . . ."

    something like that and look, I'm just going to do a little research.

CARL: So you still have more research to do . . .

DORAN: Yeah.

CARL: Wow, so you have a lot of smart plans. You want to write that lead and then, you have some material in your notebook, some entries, so that will help you as you draft, you want to kind of stretch those and write them better to write the different sections, the "bullets." These are the kinds of plans that good writers have when they start a draft.

DORAN: Yeah.

CARL: So how do you think your lead is going to go?

DORAN: Well, I guess first I'm just going to think about my angle and write about what it is, like at the beginning of the bully article it's telling about what her angle is and everything. So I guess I'd start . . . well, I wouldn't say, "My angle is about such and such,"

I'd say, "When you're getting toys, either if you're a parent buying gifts or you're a kid trying to get some toys that you're collecting, here are some tips and ways that you can get toys for good deals."

CARL: Let me tell you what I'm hearing here. In the lead of a feature article, there's that one sentence that's the heart of the whole article, where a writer tells her reader her angle on her subject, and you really have a feel for that sentence there. I want to talk about one other thing you could do. One thing I noticed about the bully article is Candace Purdom does more in her lead than what you're planning to do. The sentence you've got planned is like the one she has right here [I point to last sentence of the lead] where she goes, "Here are tips on making a tough spot easier."

DORAN: I see, but that's at the end of the lead for her.

CARL: For her it's at the end. What does she do at the beginning here?

DORAN: She kind of describes what some kids think of a big mean bully.

CARL: Yeah, and it's kind of fun to read, isn't it? "Bigger than Shaquille, meaner than the Wicked Witch of the West, scarier than a Raptor, we're talking about the school bully."

DORAN: Yeah. If I was going to take after that, I could say, "So you want to get a toy that's very expensive. But you don't have so much money. Here are . . ." I could enlarge on that, like she did there.

CARL: So what she's doing there is, she's really crafting her writing there. She's not just coming in with the nitty-gritty, she's really drawing you in. So why don't you just try today to start writing your lead, okay, and keep the bully lead in your head. She really starts by drawing you in before she gets to that angle sentence. Your angle sentence was so clear and so good. So why don't you try some of this work out in your lead today.

DORAN: Okay.

CARL: Good talking to you.

DORAN: Good talking with you, too.

Afterwards, I could name several things I did to help Doran become a better writer. By referring Doran back to a model text, I helped him teach himself that leads sometimes do several jobs—drawing the reader in and revealing the author's angle on the subject. Doran took this understanding and wrote a more sophisticated lead than he had originally planned (see Figure 1–3). I also modeled several of the questions that writers ask themselves about their writing, one general ("How's it going?") and several specific to the process of starting a

So you want to get that cool new toy, but you only have half the money? It's a major holiday and you have to buy toys for all your nephews, nieces and kids? Anyone who has ever stepped into a toystore has heard kids whinining for expensive toys, such as, "I want Pokemon Red, mom. Thats the one for me, or, "I Just have to have Nintendo 64 dad." Here are a few ways to get good deals on toys.

FIGURE 1–3 Doran's lead for his feature article

draft ("Could you tell me why you think you're ready to start your lead?" and "So you made a plan for the article?" and "So how do you think your lead is going to go?").

In just a few minutes of conversation with Doran, I was able to accomplish so much because I kept the point of the writing conference conversation in mind as we talked: helping him become a better writer. Everything I did to help Doran was something he could use for his next piece—or pieces he'll write in ten or twenty years.

Conferences Have a Predictable Structure
A good part of my day is spent in conversation: with my wife and daughter, with friends and colleagues, with perfect strangers. Rarely do I need to think about how to have a particular conversation. I just talk

to people, and as I talk, I draw upon my unconscious knowledge of how conversations go that I've been acquiring since being immersed in them the day I was born.

One of the things we all know intuitively about conversations—from listening to them and from participating in them—is that many of them have structures, or predictable ways they unfold. Different conversations have their own ways of getting started, various parts, transitions, and their own ways of closing. One of the simplest examples of a conversational structure shapes the back-and-forth we greet each other with every day.

"Hi, Teresa, how are you?" I say to my colleague when I see her in the Writing Project office.

"Fine, just fine," Teresa invariably replies. "And you?" she adds.

"Oh, I'm feeling good today. Thanks for asking."

This conversation occurs, with endless minor variations, hundreds of millions of times in the United States every day. Because each of us has been a party to it so many times, we barely have to think about what to say to each other.

Even highly complex conversations are shaped by structures. Every Thursday morning during the school year, the Reading and Writing Project staff gathers in our office at Teachers College for our weekly think tank. Having been part of these meetings now for five years, I can imagine how they're going to go even before I arrive. I know that first we'll gather in the Project library around a small table piled high with bagels and fruit. After we fill up our plates, we'll talk in twos and threes, updating each other about our lives. Then, as we seat ourselves around the big rectangular wooden table in the center of the room, Project Director Lucy Calkins will begin our group conversation. She'll ask, "So, people, what's the news?" That's her invitation for us all to share what's been happening in the schools we work in during the other days of the week. A few minutes of talk will pass by, and then Lucy will say, "So, what are we on about?"—that's the signal for our community to shift into high gear. If we've been studying a topic for the past several weeks, we'll skim over our notes, remembering where our conversation left off the previous Thursday, and then move forward with that conversation. If we have been planning to explore a new topic, a few of us will suggest possibilities, we'll choose one, and then we'll dig in.

The predictable structure of the Project's weekly conversation does several things for our think tank. Because we know in general how our discussion is going to go, we don't have to waste time each week trying to figure out what we're going to do together and how we're going to talk with each other. Instead, we move almost effortlessly into talking about the teaching of writing and reading. And because we know how our Thursday morning conversation is going to go, we prepare for that conversation during the week. For example, if I know that we're going to be talking about revision strategies, I find myself thinking about revision as I work in city classrooms, being especially attentive to students who are revising, so I have something to bring to the conversation on Thursday.

When I've watched teachers who are good at conferring, I've noticed that their conversations with students are shaped by a structure. Because these teachers know in general how they want their conversations with students to go—as do their students, once they've been in several conferences—the talk flows easily and naturally, and both the teachers and students hold up their ends of the talk.

These teachers and their students, of course, weren't born possessing a special chromosome for conferring. The teachers probably learned how a conference goes from watching their cooperating teacher confer when they were student teachers, from observing a more experienced colleague or staff developer, or from watching videotapes or studying transcripts. The students learned primarily from being immersed in the conference conversation since the first day of writing workshop.

I've noticed that the conference conversation has two parts (see Figure 1–4). Both parts grow out of the underlying purpose of a conference of helping students become better writers.

In the first part, we talk with students about the work they're doing as writers. By "work" I mean what students are doing as they write in their writers notebooks or compose drafts. Are they trying to decide what kind of writing they're going to do—a poem, a memoir, a list book? Are they trying to put spaces between their words? Are they working on a lead or ending? Are they revising? Checking for spelling?

As we talk with students about the work they are doing, our job is to make an assessment of what they are doing as writers at that moment in time. By listening carefully to their words and by reading their writing, we gather information about who students are at that moment as spellers or revisors or editors of their writing. With this information in mind, we decide what to teach them.

In the first part of my conference with Doran, for example, I put together a detailed picture of the work he was doing as a writer. I learned that he had an angle on his subject—instead of writing an "all about" toys article, he was writing about how to get the best prices on

---

THE STRUCTURE OF A WRITING CONFERENCE

- Conversation about the work the child is doing as a writer
- Conversation about how the child can become a better writer

FIGURE 1–4   The structure of a writing conference

toys. I learned that Doran was the kind of writer who envisioned how his article would be organized by making a flow chart of the sections. And Doran had a plan for his lead—to write about his angle—that he had learned from reading a published feature article.

In this conversation with Doran about his writing work, I gathered the information I needed to make a teaching decision: Doran needed help with writing a more effective lead, and I could teach him that by nudging him to closely analyze the lead of the feature article he had in mind as a model.

Once we've made our teaching decision, the first part of a conference is over. In the second part of the writing conference conversation, we talk with students about how to be better writers. In this part, we teach students to do the writing work they're doing better than they were doing it before the conference.

In the second part of my conference with Doran, we talked about the lead of the feature article he had in mind as a model for his own. From this close look, Doran was able to imagine—and write—a more complex lead. I hoped that what Doran and I had done together would enable him to do it on his own in the future whenever he was writing a lead, whether it be the lead of a feature article, a memoir, or an annual report of a company for which Doran might someday work. What we had talked about in this part of our conversation moved him closer to becoming that writer.

We Confer with Lines of Thinking in Mind

In conversations, we usually focus on a subject for a while, or even the same subject for the entire conversation. That is, we develop a line of thinking about a subject.

Sometimes we get on a line of thinking as a conversation unfolds. As my wife, Robin, and I talk about our daughter, one of us will mention something Anzia did that day—waved at her shadow, repeated several words, danced when she listened to a Beatles CD—and we'll discuss that topic for several minutes.

Other times we bring lines of thinking into conversations. When Anzia is sick, for example, the first thing that Robin or I will ask the other when we come home after work is, "How is Anzia feeling?" For the next several minutes of conversation—or several hours, depending upon the seriousness of her illness—we are on a line of thinking about Anzia's sickness.

As we confer with students, we get on a line of thinking in each conference—a line of thinking that sets the direction for the rest of the conference. It is a simple matter to look at a transcript of a conference and see what line of thinking the teacher and student were on. In my conference with Doran, for example, we got on a line of thinking about writing a lead.

What's not so obvious, however, is why a teacher and student get on one line of thinking and not another. Why is it that Doran and I talked about his lead, and not his overall plan for the piece?

We develop lines of thinking in conferences because we bring this question to them: What can I teach students about the writing work they are doing that will help them become better writers? Usually, we find the answer to this question during the first part of a conference, when students describe their writing work. For example, a child tells us about how he's editing his draft and shows us what he has done. As he talks about his editing work, we see an opportunity to teach him something about editing—an editing strategy, perhaps, or a grammar rule. All of a sudden, we're on a line of thinking with the student about that strategy or rule, and we follow that line all the way until the end of the conference.

Sometimes there are several lines of thinking we could pursue in a conference, but we have to pick one. I could have gotten on a line of thinking with Doran about his plan for his article, for example—he had a theory about how to organize the subsections of a feature article that would have been interesting to discuss—yet I chose to focus on writing a lead instead. I probably could have helped Doran become a better writer by pursuing the line of thinking about organization. But I had to make a decision, and I went with the lead because Doran wanted to get started with his draft and that's where he was directing his energy and enthusiasm. There would be opportunities to help Doran with organization in conferences later in the school year.

In other conferences, we bring lines of thinking with us into the conversations. As the year unfolds and we get to know students as individual writers, we have their strengths and weaknesses already in mind when we begin conferences. We know that in her last piece of writing, Samantha made some important revision breakthroughs. And we know from reading through the last couple of days of work in Robert's writing folder that he writes the first and last consonant sounds when he spells words. When we confer with them about their new pieces, we'll be hoping for opportunities to take Samantha deeper as a revisor and to help Robert go further with his spelling.

Some of our lines of thinking will originate out of our whole-class teaching. We choose the focus of a mini-lesson (or several consecutive mini-lessions), of course, because we have a hunch that many, if not all, of the students in our class need to learn about that subject. Naturally, we're going to be curious about the impact this whole-class teaching has on students. As we listen to them talk about their writing work, we hope that some of them will tell us about how they tried out what we talked about in our mini-lesson. We can learn how they are making sense of the lesson, and perhaps teach them more about it. With other students, we'll initiate conversations about whether or not the mini-lesson had an effect on their writing.

In Conferences, Teachers and Students Have Roles

In conversations, we play different roles. In some conversations, for example, one person leads the talk. Think of the conversation we have with a cop who has pulled us over—the officer is in charge from the beginning to the end of the exchange. He or she brings a line of thinking into the conversation ("Sir, you were going 70 in a 55 mile zone . . .") and asks us questions. It's our role to respond to the questions (and do whatever we can to convince the cop not to give us a ticket).

In other conversations, one person has the lead for awhile, then the other. When we have dinner with a friend, we might set the direction of the conversation for a time, then our friend, and so on back and forth throughout the evening. We ask our friend about how her job is going, and pursue that line of thinking with her by asking her follow-up questions; then our friend changes the subject and asks us how our children are doing, and pursues that line of thinking with us for awhile.

A writing conference is similar to this latter kind of conversation. The conference begins with students in the lead role, setting the agenda for the conversation by describing the work they are doing as writers. Then, as we get on a line of thinking about each student's work, we assume the lead, first by asking questions and reading the student's writing to help us assess what the student is doing, then by sharing our assessment with the student, and finally, by teaching.

The conference I had with Doran had this rhythm. Our conversation began with him in the lead role as he discussed his plans for starting the draft of his feature article, and the work he had done to get to this point. Then, as I got on a line of thinking with him about how he was going to write his lead, I became the conversational leader by asking him to tell me about his plan for the lead, giving him feedback about those plans, and then teaching him about how he could write a more effective lead.

Although we both lead the conversation for part of the conference, students have different conversational responsibilities than us when they're in the lead role, and also when they're not. Figure 1–5 summarizes these conversational responsibilities.

We Show That We Care

We enter into many conversations in part because we are interested in the subject, but mainly because we care about the person with whom we're talking. We talk with a close friend about the frustrations he is experiencing in locating a Manhattan apartment because we've had a similar experience and it's fun to trade horror stories—but more important because we have a genuine interest in our friend's life and its ups and downs. Over time, the subjects of our conversations will change (especially after he finally locates an apartment), but the concern we have for each other remains a constant. It's because of that concern, in fact, that we keep having conversations.

I fear that with all the pressure we feel today as teachers to raise test scores and to get our students to meet standards, it's all too easy to forget we must communicate to them in conferences how much we care about them. It's all too easy to focus so intently on the work students are doing as writers, and teaching them how to do that work better, that we see only their work, and not the young writers who are doing the work. The reason that many students are willing to take on the difficult challenge of outgrowing themselves as writers is not because we ask just the right questions about their writing work, or because our feedback is right on the mark, or because we teach them brilliantly. In the end, the success of a conference often rests on the extent to which stu-

FIRST THE STUDENT IS IN THE LEAD ROLE . . .

Student
Sets agenda for conference by describing her writing work.

Teacher
Listens carefully to what the students say about her writing work; asks questions to clarify and deepen his understanding of the student's work.

THEN THE TEACHER IS IN THE LEAD ROLE . . .

Teacher
Pursues a line of thinking about the student's writing work by asking questions and reading the student's writing.

Student
Responds to her teacher's questions.

Shares his assessment of the student's writing work.

Listens carefully to the assessment; asks questions to clarify and deepen her understanding of the assessment.

Helps student learn to do her writing work better

Tries to figure out how to do her work better, or listens carefully to what the teacher says about how to do her work better.

FIGURE 1-5   Conference Roles

dents sense that we are genuinely interested in them as writers—and as individuals.

We can all probably remember one writing teacher who inspired us to do the hard work of learning to write well. I am writing this book today, in part, because my eighth-grade teacher, Mrs. Costa, told me that she thought I would write one someday. Twenty-five years later, I don't remember the essays I wrote that year or what she said about them, nor can I name the lessons Mrs. Costa taught me about writing. I do, however, remember the personal interest she took in me as a young writer. With a few words, Mrs. Costa changed my life.

We can show students we care about them by how we talk with them about their writing work. When we ask, "How's it going?" or "What work are you doing as a writer today?" at the beginning of conferences, students can hear in our tone of voice and by the expression on our face that we really are interested in how their writing is going and the work they're doing.

As conferences unfold, we listen intently to everything students tell us about what they're doing and ask questions because we're genuinely curious to learn more about their work. Donald Graves (1983) describes how hard this listening can be:

> Listening to children is more a deliberate act than a natural one. It isn't easy to put aside personal preferences, anxieties about helping more children, or the glaring, mechanical errors that stare from the page. I mumble to myself, "Shut up, listen, and learn!" (100)

The payoff for the "deliberate act" of listening is this: we nurture the genuine connections between us and our students, and those connections have so much to do with the success of our conferences.

How we listen is that important. Writing, after all, is an individual act that occurs in a social context. That context includes not only the audience for whom we write, but the circle of mentors and friends with whom we write. For many of us who write, it's the circle of mentors and friends who help us with the difficult and often frustrating work that goes into a piece of writing, whether it's a book like this or a haiku. It's the members of that circle, after all, who listen to us while we are in the process of writing, not our future audience.

This book, for example, was born in a conversation with Randy Bomer, then co-director of the Teachers College Reading and Writing Project, over beer in a cafe on Manhattan's Upper West Side. Randy listened hard to my idea for a book, and his genuine interest in my plans gave me the courage to begin writing. As I began fleshing out my ideas in my writers notebook and starting my initial drafts, it was the thoughtful listening of my colleague Sharon Hill during long airplane trips to Columbia, Missouri, that sustained me. As I drafted and revised, the careful listening of Lucy Calkins helped me push my thinking and renewed my energy for writing. Randy, Sharon, and Lucy listened in ways that helped me feel the hard work I was doing was worth my time and effort.

Our students have the same need. By truly listening to them as we confer, we let them know that the work they're doing as writers matters. It's the way we listen, more than anything else, that will nudge our students to talk about what they're trying to do, to use the words they haven't used before, to look at us with a smile instead of a frown when we kneel down next to them and ask, "How's it going?"

As we confer, we look for opportunities to point out that students are doing good work. We say to Doran, "Wow, so you have a lot of smart plans . . . These are the kinds of plans that good writers have when they start a draft." Or we say to Amanda, "Your ending reminds me of the way Cynthia Rylant ended *When I Was Young in the Mountains.*" When children sense that we see them as intelligent people, they live up to our image of them. They feel confident in themselves, and become more willing to take the risks that we ask them to take in their writing.

We also show students that we care about them by responding to the content of their writing. When we learn that Doran is writing an article about getting good prices on toys, we let him know we are fascinated. We say, "You know, I can't believe how much toys cost, even for babies, so you're doing people like me—parents—a real service here." Or when Junior tells us he is writing a memoir about how his dad taught him to ride a bicycle, we express our interest in his experiences. We say, "What a story that is, Junior. I can tell how important your dad is to you, and how much it means to you that he took the time to teach you." When our responses communicate to students that we care about their lives, they feel motivated to do the work necessary to compose pieces of writing about those lives. Many students learn from these kinds of responses, in fact, that they have lives that are worth writing about.

A few words, a smile, a nod of understanding. That's all it takes to show students we care about them. That's all it takes to inspire some students to stretch themselves as writers. That's all it takes to change some students' writing lives.

YEARS AGO, I worried I would never have relationships with students that made a difference in their lives. When I first read about writing conferences, I realized that conferring would give me the opportunity to get to know students, and to affect their lives as writers.

It's helpful to think of writing conferences as conversations. All of us have a lifetime of experience with conversations, and these experiences have prepared us to have successful conferences. We can take what we have learned about conversation and use it to understand the characteristics of writing conferences.

References

Calkins, Lucy. 1994. *The Art of Teaching Writing.* Portsmouth, NH: Heinemann.

Graves, Donald. 1983. *Writing: Teachers & Children at Work.* Portsmouth, NH: Heinemann.

Murray, Donald M. 1985. *A Writer Teaches Writing.* Boston: Houghton Mifflin.

Purdom, Candace. 1994. "So a big, bad bully is coming after you . . ." *The Chicago Tribune, Kids News.* August 23, 1.

The Teacher's Role in the Conference 2

When I was a teenager, I was infatuated with Debbie, a pretty girl from my sailing club. Because she lived in a town ten miles from mine, we did a lot of our talking on the telephone.

Before I called Debbie, I usually made a list of things to talk about with her. After we finished talking about a topic on the list, I crossed it off and started talking about the next one.

Alas, Debbie never returned my feelings for her. Looking back, I can see I didn't understand the role a suitor plays in a conversation with the object of his affection. Talking about topics on a list, as it turned out, wasn't the best strategy for drawing Debbie out and demonstrating I was interested in her and what was going on in her life. Had I put less energy into figuring out *what* I was going to say and, instead, put more into learning *how* to have a good conversation with her, perhaps we would have become more than "just friends."

For us to have successful writing conferences, we too should worry less about what we're going to talk about with students. When I first started conferring, I was so worried my students and I would have nothing to say to each other that I memorized lists of the "right" subjects to talk about and the "right" questions to ask them. Unfortunately, since these subjects and questions often had little to do with the writing work my students were actually doing, the lists got in the way of our having worthwhile conversations.

I finally realized that my role in a conference is to find out *from students* what work they are doing as writers and then teach them how to do that work better. Instead of worrying about what I was going to talk about with them, I concentrated on learning how to have conversations in which students tell me what they need, and I meet those needs.

The focus of this chapter is on our role as teachers in the writing conference conversation. (See Figure 2–1.) Since the writing conference conversation has two parts to it—the first, in which we talk with students about the work they're doing as writers, and the second, in which we talk with them about how to become better writers—I have

THE TEACHER'S ROLE IN A CONFERENCE

In the first part of the conversation:
- invite the student to set an agenda for the conference
- get on a line of thinking about the student's writing work by asking research questions and reading the student's writing
- decide what to teach the student

In the second part of the conversation:
- give the student critical feedback
- teach the student
- nudge the student to have-a-go
- link the conference to the student's independent work

FIGURE 2-1   The teacher's role in a conference

included a section on each part. In each section, I discuss the conversational moves we make when we have successful conversations with students about their writing. I also discuss the intellectual work that we need to do in order to realize our goal of helping students become better writers.

I have also included sections on how to deal with two kinds of conferences that teachers find particularly challenging. In one, I discuss conferences in which we decide not to focus on the work students tell us they are doing. And in the second, I talk about conferring with students who tell us they are finished with their drafts.

The Teacher's Role in the First Part of the Writing Conference
In the first part of a writing conference, we have a conversation with students about the work they're doing at that point in time in their writ-

ing. That is, we talk about their intentions—*what* they're doing—and their strategies for realizing those intentions—*how* they're doing what they're doing. In a conference with a first grader, for example, we might talk about how she's trying to write an unfamiliar word—that's her intention—and how she's sounding out the word and writing the letters that correspond to the sounds she hears—that's the strategy she's using. Or in a conference with a fifth grader, we might talk about how he's trying to craft a good lead to his memoir—that's his intention—and how he's studying the leads of his favorite memoirists in order to use them as models for his own—that's the strategy he's using. (See Figure 2–2.)

Because writers do different kinds of work at different points in the writing process—rehearsal, drafting, revising, and editing—conferences focus on different issues at each point.

1. In *rehearsal* conferences, we help students find ideas to write about, or gather the information they need to write drafts. In many writing workshops, students do this work in their writers notebooks.
2. In *drafting* conferences, we assist students with developing the big idea that frames their pieces, deciding which genre and structure to write in, developing content, crafting their writing, or keeping words flowing.
3. In *revision* conferences, we focus on helping students improve their drafts. We help students clarify their big ideas, consider whether their writing reflects the qualities of the genre in which they are writing, rethink their structures, add on or delete content, craft their writing, or make sure that their writing makes sense.
4. In *editing* conferences, we help students become better editors. We talk with them about editing strategies, or we discuss the conventions of the language—grammar, mechanics, and spelling.

During the first part of the conference, we make several conversational moves. First we invite the student to set the agenda for the conference by describing the writing work she's doing. Then we assume the lead role in the conversation by getting on a line of thinking about her work. We do this by asking her questions and looking at her writing.

As we talk with the student about her writing, we do crucial intellectual work. We make an assessment of how well she is doing her writing work, and we decide what we're going to teach her to help her learn to do that work better.

EXAMPLES OF THE KINDS OF WORK THAT WRITERS DO
WHEN THEY COMPOSE PIECES

When Writers Have This Intention . . .	*They Might Use One of These Strategies*
Find an idea to write about	Freewriting Look around and let objects spark ideas
Figure out the focus for a piece	Ask themselves, "What's the thing I really want to say about my subject to readers?"
Organize a draft	Study the structure of a model piece Make a flow chart of the piece
Write an ending	Study the endings of several model pieces Brainstorm several endings and pick the one that works best
Add information to a draft	Read the piece to someone and add information that person wants to know Draw a picture of what they're writing about to help them think of what else they could say
Edit their drafts	Read their pieces out loud to themselves Read their pieces out loud to someone else

FIGURE 2–2   Examples of the kinds of work that writers do

Our first job is to invite students to set the agenda for the conference. We do this by asking them an open-ended question. Some of these questions include:

- How's it going?
- What are you doing today as a writer?
- What work are you doing as a writer this period?
- What do you need help with today?

Although these are my favorite opening questions, I don't think that they are the *open sesames* of conferring that are guaranteed to get children talking about their writing work. In fact, I don't think it matters too much which opening lines I actually use, as long as they're open-ended—and that, over time, I use them over and over again to start my conferences. It's the repetition that cues students to talk about their writing work, not the questions themselves. When I begin a conference with "How's it going?"—just as I have in the last conference and the conference before that—I'm reminding a student of how those conversations went. By using a predictable opening, I'm simply taking advantage of students' implicit knowledge of the nature of conversation, and that some conversations begin in predictable ways.

I was reminded of the importance of using predictable openings while working in Andrea Clark's fourth-grade classroom at Derby Ridge Elementary in Columbia, Missouri. My first conferences, which I began with "How's it going?" all started off poorly. The students looked confused and fell silent. I was puzzled, and a little bit embarrassed, too, since Andrea had been bragging to me about how well her kids had learned to talk with her about their writing. Finally, in the middle of another long silence, I turned and asked Andrea which opening she used. She told me she usually began conferences by asking, "What are you doing today as a writer?" Before I could get the words out of my mouth, the student I was trying to confer with perked right up and began to talk about her writing work.

In many writing workshops, once the school year is under way and students have been in several conferences, we don't even need to ask an opening question. Our sitting down next to students becomes their cue to start talking about their writing work.

As students talk about their writing work, thereby setting the agenda for the conference, we listen carefully to what they're saying. Of course, some of our students are not able to talk about their writing work with much sophistication. It's part of our role, then, to support their talk. Because this talk is such an important source of information, I have devoted Chapter 3 to a discussion of how to teach students to talk well about what they're doing as writers.

Let's take a look at a conference in which a student set the conference agenda. It was an early October morning in Jennifer Geller's second-grade classroom at P.S. 6 in Manhattan. We knelt down to confer with Becky, who was working on revising her story about her sleepover party (see Figure 2–3).

CARL: How's it going?

BECKY: Well, I'm revising "My Sleepover." This part, "We made popcorn without butter." I added on, "It was good."

CARL: [I skim Becky's work and notice that she also added on "It was good," to the part about eating pizza.] So you're revising "My Sleepover." You added on to two parts in your story—using the arrow strategy I showed your class. Tell me a little bit about how you're using the strategy.

BECKY: The arrows . . . drawing them helps me remember the part I'm stretching, remember what I can add on.

CARL: So when you draw an arrow, that helps you think of what you can add on?

BECKY: Yeah.

CARL: So why did you pick these places to stretch?

BECKY: Because there was something . . . like . . . something more I could say.

CARL: Becky, one thing I'm curious about. You wrote, "We made popcorn. It was good." It was *good*?

BECKY: When I said it was good, I mean it was *yum*.

At this point, the first part of the conference was over. I turned to Ms. Geller and named what had happened so far in the conversation. In response to my opening question, Becky had done a beautiful job of talking about her writing work, using words like *revising* and *added on*. Becky's talk about her revision work set the conference's direction from the start. I immediately got on a line of thinking about her adding on, and was now ready to teach her how to do this work better. I turned back to Becky and resumed the conference.

CARL: Becky, I'm really impressed that you made two revisions to your piece. I want to talk to you about how you can revise even better. Remember when I showed you my piece about my two cats? Remember how I stretched "My cats were sitting on the windowsill"

My Sleepover (Becky)

Friday night I had a sleepover with Jessy, Molly and Lexi Hart. Jessy is eight, Molly is seven and Lexi is five. We made popcorn without butter. We watched a few movies like

it was good

Matilda, Spice World and Toy Story. We had pizza for dinner at Little Robins right across the street and down a little bit. They

it was good

live in Scarsdale. I don't know what part of Scarsdale. Well.....
at least we had a GREAT TIME!

FIGURE 2–3   First draft of Becky's "My Sleepover"

by writing, "They were sitting so still, they looked like statues. Only their tails moved." Would you have been able to see what my cats looked like if I had just said, "My cats were sitting on the windowsill. *They looked good*"?

BECKY: [shakes her head]

CARL: I didn't give you much there, did I?

BECKY: No.

CARL: Becky, when you wrote, "We made popcorn. It was good," I have no idea of what you mean by "good."

BECKY: So I should just erase that?

CARL: [I chuckle.] No, no . . . What I'm going to do is help you to add on in a way that will help us understand what you mean by "good" when we read your piece. One thing that writers do when they're revising a piece is try to get a picture of what they're writing about in their heads. When I do this, and I can really "see" what I'm writing about in my mind, that helps me think of details I can add to my piece. I'm going to have you try that. Which of these parts—the popcorn or the pizza—do you want to work on some more?

BECKY: The popcorn.

CARL: So can you see that popcorn in your head?

BECKY: Well, most of the time when I'm writing I actually get it onto the piece better than I talk.

CARL: I want you to talk it out right now, practice it before you write it. Talk about that popcorn.

BECKY: Well, it's like fresh popcorn, I just got it from the store, my dad just got it from the store . . .

CARL: Fresh popcorn from the store . . . and . . .

BECKY: And . . . and it's only one type of popcorn . . . it was plain . . .

CARL: You're saying so much more than just, "It was good." [I say back to Becky what I heard her say about making popcorn.] *You made popcorn without butter. It was the plain popcorn fresh from the store.* When you said all that, I had a better sense of what you meant by "It was good."

BECKY: So I could add that to my story?

CARL: That's a great idea. You could also look at the other place where you added on and see if you could write more than "It was good" in the same way that you did with me.

BECKY: Okay.

CARL: You're working really hard, Becky. You're doing something writers do when they revise—they really try to help us get a picture of what they're writing about. I'll check back later in the period to see how you make out with this work.

When Ms. Geller and I checked in with Becky at the end of the workshop, we were pleased to see that she had reworked the part of her story about making popcorn that we had talked about in the conference and the part about eating pizza, too (see Figure 2–4). She had successfully tried writing with detail instead of using the word *good*.

As a child describes her writing work in the beginning of a conference, I ask myself, "Do I 'get behind'—that is, support—the writing work that this student is telling me she is doing?" I prefer to get behind the student's agenda and teach her how to do better the work she is already doing. The conference I had with Becky, for example, was one in which I got behind her adding on work. Since it's my goal to help students become writers who have their own intentions, it makes sense to support those intentions whenever possible. And if I help a student with work that she has decided to do on her own, then it's more likely that she'll be motivated to try out what I teach her.

To help me decide whether or not I should get behind what a student tells me she is doing as a writer, I consider what I know about what she needs to grow as a writer. Once the school year is under way and I've had several conferences with each student in the class and read their writing, I have a sense of each child's strengths, as well as what they need to grow as writers. And in each subsequent conference, I learn more about each student's strengths and needs. When I confer with students, I am hoping to find opportunities to teach them what I think they need as individual writers.

In many conferences, then, I get behind what a child tells me she's doing as a writer not only to support her agenda, but because getting behind this writing work gives me the chance to teach her something I know she needs to learn. In my conference with Becky, I decided to teach her about adding on to her draft not just because she chose to do this work on her own, but because I knew from her teacher that Becky had been the kind of student who had previously seen revision as fixing up spelling and punctuation. Her willingness to add on represented a significant breakthrough for her.

When I'm considering whether or not to get behind a student's agenda, I also consider what I've been focusing on in recent mini-lessons. When I've given several mini-lessons on a particular topic and then have the chance to follow up on that topic in conferences, students will have some familiarity with what I'm teaching them individually.

① <u>My Sleepover</u> (Becky)

Friday night I had a sleepover with Jessy, molly and Lexi Hart. Jessy is eight, Molly is seven and Lexi is five. We made popcorn without butter. It was fresh from the store. The popcorn was only one flavor. Orignal was the flavor..... my favorite kind! We watched a few movies like Matilda and Toy Story. We had pizza for dinner at Little Robins pizza place right across the street. Everybody had plain pizza except me. I had

FIGURE 2–4   Second draft of Becky's "My Sleepover"

② **My Sleepover** Becky

Mushroom pizza and except for my mom and dad too. They ate when everybody was asleep. The Hart's live in Scarsdale. I don't know what part of Scarsdale. But they are very, very, very nice and fun people and best of all.... WE HAD A GREAT TIME!!!!!

FIGURE 2–4 *(Continued)*

Also, when I've taught several mini-lessons on the same topic, then many of the students in the class will be trying out what I've been talking about in those mini-lessons. If I connect my conference teaching to these mini-lessons, when I finish these conferences students will be able to have peer conferences with other students in the class who are doing the same work, and get support from them when I am not available. In many conferences—the ones I had with Becky, for example—the writing work that students tell us they are doing is inspired by mini-lessons. In these conferences, I almost always get behind this work.

However, in many other conferences, students tell us about writing work they are doing that *doesn't* match what we are talking about in mini-lessons. In these conferences, I have to resist the temptation to

35

ignore the students' agenda and immediately change the subject of the conference to what I have been talking about in mini-lessons. In these conferences, I have to step back and ask myself what's best for the student, not what might be easiest for me to teach.

Although we prefer to get behind students' agendas for their writing, we sometimes decide not to focus on the work they tell us they are doing. Later on in the chapter, I discuss these kinds of conferences.

Get On a Line of Thinking About Students' Writing Work
We rarely get all of our information in conversations from what a partner tells us. Her body language, as well as her tone of voice, also give us information. Sometimes the words she says, her body language, and her tone of voice are all in sync. She says her life is going well in a cheerful voice, and as she talks she holds her head and shoulders up high. Other times, however, a person gives us conflicting messages. She says she's fine, yet her eyes are sad, and she hangs her head. We weigh all of this information as we talk.

As we confer, we assess what a student can do as a writer at that moment in time by considering several sources of information. What a student says about his writing at the beginning of the conversation is the most obvious source. There are several reasons, however, why what a child tells us about his writing work may not give us enough of the information we need to make an accurate assessment. Some children give us an incomplete picture of the work they're doing. Other children do the best they can to describe their writing work, but they can't talk about their work with the degree of metacognition that experienced adult writers can. And what some children tell us doesn't match the work they have actually done or can do as writers.

For all of these reasons, once a student has set the agenda for the conference—and we've decided to get behind the work he's doing—we take the lead in the conversation by getting on a line of thinking about his work. We ask the student research questions—questions that nudge him to say more about his writing work. And we read his writing.

In a conference with Nick, a student in Roy Silverstein's fifth-grade class at P.S. 6, I pursued a line of thinking about the "envisionment" work he was doing as he began writing a short story. That is, I gathered information about what Nick thought his story was going to be about, and how he was going to tell that story. Nick had spent a week writing in his writers notebook about his main character, Timmy. This work had helped Nick get to know the character and the issues in the character's life. Just before we conferred, Nick had figured out what story he wanted to tell about Timmy, and had just begun writing it.

CARL: So could you tell me what work you're doing as a writer today?

NICK: Well, right now I'm starting on the draft . . . I'm just kind of putting everything together to make the story.

CARL: *What do you mean, "putting everything together"?*

NICK: All the entries I wrote about Timmy—he's my main character—in my notebook. Timmy's mom is sick. His friends, they're not really friends, so when they find out that his mother's sick, and they kind of feel bad for him, and he gets a little closer to them. And he also gets a little closer to his mother, when she gets better.

CARL: It seems to me that you've been thinking hard about what story you're going to tell about Timmy. *What's the problem, the issue Timmy's going to resolve in this story?*

NICK: Well, he doesn't really have close friends. He's sort of just left out.

CARL: *So what does Timmy need?*

NICK: Well, he hasn't really like told his friends yet, and so they don't really understand it, and so he kinda acts a little different. He needs to tell them, I guess.

CARL: It seems like the issue you want Timmy to grapple with is his relationships with his friends.

NICK: Uh-huh.

CARL: *Can I see what you've written?* [I read the two paragraphs Nick has written so far. See Figure 2–5.]

I stopped the conference and I analyzed what had happened so far in the conversation. I pointed out to Mr. Silverstein how Nick had set the agenda for this conference when he said he was "putting everything together to make the story"—that is, Nick was deciding what problem he wanted his main character to grapple with. I decided to get behind Nick's agenda, I explained, since the decision about what big idea to focus on has so much to do with writing a successful piece.

I said I had got on a line of thinking about Nick's work first by asking him several research questions. When I asked the first, "What do you mean, 'putting everything together'?" I was trying to nudge Nick to elaborate on his response to my opening question. Nick's response concerned me. It seemed he was planning to tell a story in which his main character faced several problems (his mother's sickness, the difficulty of opening up to his friends, and his relationship with his mother), in contrast to the short stories Nick and his classmates had been reading,

P.S. 6.
5-301

Nick
4/30/99

Timmy sat in his bed, staring
at the ceiling covered with plastic
glow-in-the-dark stars which shined
against the pale background. "Why did
my mom out of all the others have to
get sick," he said to himself.
    Timmy was very unhappy because
of his mother's disease. She had been
in the hospital for almost a month and
missed her very much. He pulled himself
out of bed and walked to the living room
where he plopped himself on the couch.
His father handed him some cereal
which got him into a better mood.

FIGURE 2–5   Nick's first lead for his short story

in which the main character faced one problem. So I asked Nick two follow-up questions—"What's the problem, the issue Timmy's going to resolve in this story?" and "So what does Timmy need?" In response, Nick told me his story was going to be about Timmy learning how to open up to his friends.

Then, I said, I looked at what Nick had written so far. As I read, it struck me that what Nick seemed to be setting up in the beginning was a story about Timmy dealing with his mother's sickness, not a story about getting closer to friends. I decided that what I needed to teach Nick in this conference was how to set up the problem in its opening section.

CARL: You know, when I read what you've written so far, I don't really get a sense this is going to be a story about a boy who has trouble with his friends. From what you've written, my sense of the story is that it's about a boy dealing with his mom's illness.

NICK: Yeah, but this is only just the very beginning.

CARL: I understand that. Nick, what I want to talk with you about today is how many short story writers set up the main character's problem right at the beginning of a story. Remember how in the first paragraph of "Spaghetti" [by Cynthia Rylant] you found out that Gabriel wishes for some company? Remember how in the first *sentence* of "The New Kid" [by Dori Butler] you find out Kayla hated being the new kid in school? What does Timmy feel about his friends?

Nick: Well, yeah, but Timmy doesn't think about his friends very much.

CARL: Think about Gabriel. Does he know he's lonely in "Spaghetti"?

NICK: Yeah.

CARL: How does Kayla feel about being the new kid in school?

NICK: She hates it.

CARL: So both characters are aware of their feelings. I think that given these stories are your models, it seems like Timmy should be aware of his feelings about his friends to some extent. I'd like you to try setting up his problem early, like these writers did. How do you think you could do that?

NICK: Well . . . I could maybe just start it at school where his friends are.

CARL: You could start the story at school? That's a great idea, to try a different lead to set the problem up.

NICK: Well, he'd probably be unhappy about his mom and then his friends might . . . you know . . . ask him to like play something with them and he might . . . you know . . . he might say no . . .

CARL: He acts a little weird with them? How do they react to him, then?

NICK: They probably just leave him.

CARL: Wow, if you start that way, it really sets Timmy's problem up well. So try that. Skip a line and freewrite some of that right now. Go for it.

Later on in the period, Mr. Silverstein and I dropped by Nick's table to see how he had made out with reworking his lead section. We were impressed by what he had written (see Figure 2–6). In the new version, Nick had tried successfully to set up Timmy's problem in the very first paragraph of the story.

P.S.6.   Nick
5-301   4/30/99

<u>Tim's Not-Really Friends</u>
    Tim dropped his backpack on one
of the green school benches and sat
down. His not-really friends came over.
"I've got a baseball," one said. "No thanks,"
Tim replied. It was all because of his
mother. Oh why did she have to get
sick?
    In class Timmy didn't pay as
close attention as he normally did.
Timmy," went the squeaky voice of
Ms. Opentili, the 6th grade math teacher.
"What is the answer to problem 3?"
Timmy lifted his head from his desk
and reluctantly answered the problem.
"Good," responded the teacher.
    The rest of the day Tim sat at
his desk, staring at his pencil. Even during
recess he didn't bother asking his friends
if he could play. They wouldn't care
either. No one knew how miserable he was.
Meanwhile his friends were talking. "Why
is that kid just sitting over there?" said
one. Another answered "Oh, he's just weird,
he never made any sense."

FIGURE 2–6   Nick's revised lead

Ask Research Questions   As we get on a line of thinking about a student's writing work, what research questions should we ask her?

When I ask research questions, I try to remember that my job as a writing teacher is to help students become better writers, not to improve the pieces of writing they are currently working on. It's all too easy to ask leading questions that inadvertently direct students to develop content or to arrive at meanings that are ours and not necessarily theirs. Let's say we learn that a fourth grader is in the middle of a piece about how his uncle showed him how to fly kites and throw a football. It may seem obvious to us that the child's uncle was like a teacher to him, and so we are tempted to ask, "So is your big idea that your uncle is an important teacher to you?" We resist this temptation because we know that the student may say yes simply to please us, even though he hasn't yet thought about his big idea or even if his big idea is actually that he misses his uncle, who lives far away in Puerto Rico, because they do many fun things together when he visits New York City. Instead, we ask, "So what's the big idea of your piece?" When we ask research questions in this open-ended manner, we give students the freedom to answer honestly, without fear of displeasing us.

Open-ended research questions *do* lead students, but toward an understanding of what good writers do. When we ask, "So what's the big idea of your piece?" we are implicitly letting students know that pieces have big ideas. As a writing teacher, I want to lead students toward these kinds of understandings, and open-ended research questions help me do this.

It's important to understand there is no generic list of research questions we can memorize and ask in every conference. The specific questions we ask students, in fact, differ from conference to conference, depending on the students, the kind of writing work they are doing, and what they say about their work. Even when two students are both doing the same kind of writing work, we may ask them different questions because they are different writers.

There are, however, certain *kinds* of questions that we ask over and over again in conferences, no matter what kind of work students are doing and what kind of writers they are. Each of these kinds of questions helps us gather information about the writing work students are doing, either by nudging students to say more about the work they told us at the beginning of the conference, or by eliciting information that they didn't tell us.

Research questions, I've found, fall into the following six categories.

Questions That Nudge Students to Say More
- "Could you say more about that?"
- "What do you mean by . . ."
- "Could you explain what you mean by . . ."

When students describe their writing work, they often don't give us the detail we need to help us get a complete picture of what they're doing. We say to ourselves, "I have a general sense of what she's doing, but I need more information to really understand." For example, when Nick said that he was "putting everything together to make the story," I was hungry for more detail about his envisionment work. Consequently, I asked him, "What do you mean, 'putting everything together'?"

Questions That Grow Out of Our Knowledge of What Good Writers Do
- "Have you planned out your draft?"
- "What's the focus of your piece?"
- "What kinds of revisions have you made?"

In conferences when students tell me *in general* what they're doing ("I'm starting a draft," "I'm revising," etc.), I try to get them to elaborate by asking them if they've done any of the kinds of work that good writers usually do at the same juncture of the writing process. Because I write, and because I have read numerous books on writing, I have developed a sense for the different kinds of things writers do as they rehearse their ideas, draft, revise, and edit. I know, for example, that when many writers start drafts, they decide what the focus of their piece will be, they decide which genre they will write in, and they decide how they want to structure their pieces. In my conference with Nick, as I listened to him talk about putting his short story together, I began to wonder about which problem his main character was going to face. I knew to ask that question because I've asked it myself when I've written short stories, and because I have read about how some of my favorite authors have grappled with the same issue in their writing.

Questions About Students' Writing Strategies
- "How are you going to do this work?"
- "What strategies are you going to use to do this work?"
- "How are you planning to get started with your draft?"

Sometimes students tell me what they're doing, or what they want to do, but they don't tell me *how* they're doing this work. For example, a child tells me that he is editing but doesn't tell me that he has been reading the piece out loud to himself, or plans to have a classmate read the piece with him. I need to know this kind of information to help me assess what kind of editor he is.

Questions That Come from What We Already Know About Students
- "Have you done some of the revision work you tried in your last piece?"
- "How did you pick the idea for your draft this time?"

Some of the questions I ask children grow out of what I already know about them as writers. As I get to know students, both from conferring with them and from reading their writing, I develop a sense for which writing issues each of them is grappling with at that point in his development as a writer. When I talk with them in subsequent conferences, I'll be wondering about how they are handling those issues. One logical question to ask Nick in subsequent conferences, for example, would be, "How have you set up your big idea this time?"

Questions Connected to Our Mini-Lessons
- "Have you tried out what we talked about today in the mini-lesson?"
- "Remember how we talked yesterday in the mini-lesson about revision strategies? Have you used any of them to help you revise?"

Some of the questions I ask grow directly out of the mini-lesson I taught that day, or on a previous day. The reason I give a particular mini-lesson, of course, is because I feel that many of the students in the class need to learn what I'm teaching. Once I've taught the lesson, I'm naturally curious about whether or not the students are using what I taught them in their writing.

Let's say I've noticed that a number of students are getting stuck in the middle of a draft and are having trouble getting restarted. In response, I give a mini-lesson on how to reread what you've written so far as a way to get going again. If I subsequently have a conference with a student who is stuck, then I'll be curious about whether or not he used the rereading strategy, and if he did, whether or not the strategy helped him.

Questions About a Student's Decisions
- "Why did you pick these places to add-on?"
- "Why did you decide to structure your draft this way?"
- "Why did you repeat this line several times?"

As I confer, I sometimes wonder *why* a student made the decisions he has made in the process of writing his piece. For example, I may want to know why he chose the topic he's writing about. Or why he chose to develop some scenes and not others. Or why he chose to use a semicolon in a sentence. Finding out why a student made a particular decision—whether the student gives me an explanation himself in the course of our conversation about his writing work, or I have to ask him myself—helps me understand how deeply he understands the work he's doing.

Look at Students' Writing   To help us develop a line of thinking about a student's writing work, we also look at the writing. We can learn a great deal from looking at entries in a child's writers notebook or a draft.

I've found that how I look at a child's writing can help me make an accurate assessment of that child. Or it can sidetrack a conference, and even bring it to a halt. Most important, I don't usually read a child's entire piece during a conference. Especially with older children, it would simply take too long for me to read their pieces from beginning to end, and then I would only have one or two conferences during each writing workshop.

Instead, I look at what a child has written with my line of thinking about him as my lens. I might ask him, for example, to show me the part or the places in his draft where he is doing the work he is telling me about. When I don't have a line of thinking in mind as I look at a student's draft, I get sidetracked by any glaring errors that stand out in the piece, especially the ones that my high school English teachers told me to never, ever make in a piece of writing. I might spend the rest of the conference getting the student to fix those glaring errors instead of teaching the child what he really needs to help him become a better writer.

Nick, of course, only had two paragraphs written when I conferred with him. But even if he'd had ten pages completed, I would still only have needed to read those first two paragraphs to see how he had set up his story. My line of thinking would have kept me from reading the whole draft.

What do we do if the student hasn't yet done the work he tells us he is doing? He is thinking about how to end his memoir, for example, but hasn't yet put words down on the page that we can read. In these conferences, I ask students to do the writing *orally*. I'll say, "Could you tell me how you think your ending is going to go?" In my conference with Doran in Chapter 1, for example, I asked him to write the lead to his feature article orally:

CARL: So how do you think your lead is going to go?

DORAN: Well, I guess first I'm just going to think about my angle and write about what it is, like at the beginning of the [Candace Purdom] article it's telling about what her angle is and everything. So I guess I'd start . . . well, I wouldn't say, "My angle is about such and such," I'd say, "When you're getting toys, either if you're a parent buying gifts or you're a kid trying to get some toys that you're collecting, here are some tips and ways that you can get toys for good deals."

Listening to Doran's oral "draft" gave me the information I needed to assess what he knew about writing leads for feature articles, and to make a decision about what to teach him.

Decide What to Teach

We pursue our line of thinking about a student's writing work until we have the information we need to decide what we're going to teach a child. With this decision made, the first part of the conference is over.

How do we decide exactly what we should teach a child to help him become a better writer? It's here at this point in the conference that we do some of our most challenging intellectual work. To decide, we draw upon several sources of knowledge:

- what we know about good writing
- what we know about the writing process
- what we know about children and how they grow and develop as writers
- what we've learned about the student as a writer so far in the conference, as well as in our previous conferences with her

We consider all of this knowledge to help us make a teaching decision that matches the individual needs of the student with whom we are conferring.

One day when I was visiting Anna Lee's eighth-grade classroom in M.S. 51 in Brooklyn, we paid special attention to the teaching decision. Before conferring with William, I reviewed my conference notes to see what we had talked about the week before. William had written a draft of an editorial in which he expressed his frustration with adults who say, "That's life, get used to it." To support his point of view, he told a story about the problems he had had with a science project (see Figure 2–7). William and I had talked about how in the editorials his class had read, the authors had included several stories to support their opinions.

Almost every adult I know says "That's life, get used to it" when they are doing something unfair to me. I really hate that saying. Adults sometimes use that as an excuse to do something unfair to you. How would they like it if I didn't let them do something they wanted to do? And to top it off, what if I said "That's life, get used to it?" They would want to hunt me down like an animal. That is exactly what I want to do when someone says that to me.

One time when I was in the seventh grade, it was time to pick a partner for the yearly science fair. You could only pick one partner. I picked a friend of mine (I don't want to mention any names because it would just embarrass that person.) as my partner. That was my first mistake. As a lesson to all teenagers who are about to pick a partner for a major project, never pick a friend who you can't depend on . . .

I alone picked a topic, researched the topic, typed up a full report on the topic and out of my own pocket, paid for the presentation board. All he did was give me about $3.00 and that was it. I tried telling my science teacher that my partner wasn't doing anything. Guess what my science teacher said. "Well, that's life for you." Those few words pushed me over the edge . . .

To top it off, on the day me and my partner were supposed to present our project, he was absent . . . I stood in front of my entire class alone and presented my science project. I really hate presenting to my class. Most people are shy so they don't feel comfortable standing in front of a large group of people and talking to them. I am one of those people.

After I finished presenting, my teacher and a couple of students asked me questions. I didn't know the answers to those questions. I

FIGURE 2–7 William's first draft

just stood in front of my entire class without saying a word. It was so quiet in that room you could hear an ant crawl across the floor. After about 5 minutes (which seemed like years to me) the bell rang and the silence turned into a variety of noises.

I gathered up my belongings and walked over to my science teacher. He gave me my report and just walked away without saying a word. I got an 80. It wasn't such a bad grade but I thought I should have gotten something higher. My science teacher knew I was the one who did all the work.

The next day, I asked him if my partner would get an 80 for the science project. He said yes. That one word hit me like a ton of bricks. I did the entire science project by myself. I presented my project to the entire class by myself. So the right thing should have been that I myself got all of the credit.

But that didn't happen. Me and my science teacher argued for a few minutes over this issue. I told him my partner never lifted a finger to help me during the two months I worked hard on the project. I told him I put in my share and his share of the work and money into the project.

He just kept saying that I, not him, chose my partner. I admitted to him that I had made a big mistake but he wouldn't change his mind. My partner still got an 80 for the report. At the end, I told him this wasn't fair. His reply was, "That's life. Get used to it." I was then ready to go crazy.

I really, really hate people who use the term "That's life, get used to it." The only reason these people use this term is to do something totally unfair to you and then use this as an excuse.

FIGURE 2–7   (*Continued*)

William had said he wanted to add more stories to his draft to give his opinion more support.

CARL: How's it going?

WILLIAM: It's okay . . . I have my opinion in the beginning. Then I have my long story. I haven't added in my other two stories yet.

CARL: Let me see . . . last time we talked, you had one long story about what happened during the science project that shows why you really, really hate when people use that phrase, "That's life, get used to it." So you want to add some more stories. Your stories? Or other people's?

WILLIAM: I interviewed two people.

CARL: Can I see that?

WILLIAM: [turns to the pages in his writers notebook where he wrote down his interview notes] The questions are right here, and what they said. [See Figure 2–8.]

CARL: Okay, you asked some questions and you got some good information.

WILLIAM: Yeah.

CARL: So the work you're doing is to turn your interview notes into stories that will help us understand your opinion. You have all this stuff that people said . . . how are you going to take it and write it in draft form?

WILLIAM: Instead of questions and answers, I'm going to make them into stories by adding details.

CARL: Adding details . . . what do you mean by that?

WILLIAM: [shrugs]

At this point in the conference, I knew what I wanted to teach William. I turned to Ms. Lee to explain how I had arrived at my decision.

First, I said, I thought William needed help with how to take the information he had gathered in his interviews and put it all together to make the stories he wanted to add to his draft. I wanted to teach William how to write stories that were a mixture of narration and quotation.

I explained to Ms. Lee that I made this decision in part because of what I knew about the ways editorials are written, both from reading them on the op-ed page of *The New York Times* and other newspapers, and also from writing several myself. I know that writers such as Anna Quindlen tell stories that support their point of view by mixing narration and quotation. William had the raw materials to tell stories the same way.

Interview with Daryl J.

1. In your life, have you ever had anyone say, "That's life, get used to it" to you or something similar to that?

Yes. My uncle said it.

2. What was the situation?

Fighting. Me and my uncle. The small sink. I wanted to use it. He wanted to use it. Argument. Then dad came. Broke it up. Lectured me on fighting.

3. How did you feel afterward?

Bad. Cause of my uncle. My mom says to respect my elders. I disobeyed her. Result! Nobody got to use the sink.

4. Do you think it was fair or unfair? Why?

Unfair that he said it. Because he is older than me and he used it as an excuse to take advantage of me. Tells me what to do and wants me to do it.

5. How do you feel about this saying? Do you hate it? Do you think adults use it as an excuse sometimes?

A lot. On occasion. Sometimes not often.

6. Have you ever said this to someone else? Why?

No

FIGURE 2–8   William's interview notes

Also factoring into my decision, I said, was what I had learned about William as a writer when I looked at his draft the week before. I had noticed that in telling the story of his ill-fated science project, he had skillfully woven together narration, dialogue, and reflection. I felt confident William could tackle telling other people's stories by mixing narration and quotations.

Finally, I told Ms. Lee I had conferred with eighth graders similar to William who had been trying to do the same work. They had responded well to my teaching, and had successfully told stories using narration and quotations.

I turned back to William and began to teach.

CARL: William, I get the sense that you aren't exactly sure how you can turn your notes into stories. Am I right?

WILLIAM: I guess.

CARL: So let's talk about how you can write these stories. Which piece has your class read that used interviews?

WILLIAM: "The Police Bullies"? [by *The New York Times* columnist Bob Herbert; see Figure 2–9]

CARL: That would be a good one to look at. [I wait while William locates his copy of the editorial.] One thing you can do is read the stories that Bob Herbert tells in this piece and notice how he put them together. Could you tell me what you notice about that first section?

WILLIAM: Well, he [Bob Herbert] tells part of the story, and then Francisco tells part of the story . . . he [Herbert] uses quotes that he took from interviews.

CARL: Anything else you notice about the way it's put together?

WILLIAM: Detail. [he reads aloud] "[H]e was riding his bicycle home from work, and an unmarked car cut him off on Linden Boulevard in Queens."

CARL: So you're noticing how much information you get in a sentence. So it seems like your sentences will also need to be jam-packed with detail. You learn a lot about the story in just four, five paragraphs. So those are some things that could guide you as you write. Let's tell me how you're going to start yours. First, what's the story about?

WILLIAM: My friend's uncle. He and his uncle were fighting over the sink [chuckles]. He wanted to use it, his uncle wanted to use it, and then they were arguing. During the argument, his uncle said, "Well, that's life." His uncle thought since he was older, he could tell him what to do, and he thinks he will do it.

Francisco Maldonado, who is 19, remembers the night last summer when he was riding his bicycle home from work and plainclothes cops in an unmarked car cut him off on Linden Boulevard in Queens.

"They stopped right in front of me," he said. "The cop on the passenger side came out real fast with his gun drawn. He told me to keep my hands up. I was straddling my bike and had my book bag on my back. Then the driver came around and shouted, 'Don't move!'"

"I was so frightened. I thought I was going to get shot. When they were talking to me, I was shaking."

The cops looked Mr. Maldonado over and then told him he was free to go. They said someone had reported a bike stolen in the area.

Still frightened, Mr. Maldonado nevertheless ventured a question. "I said, 'Why did you have to come out right away with that gun drawn like that and scare me like you did?' He said, 'That's none of your business.'"

FIGURE 2–9   First section of Bob Herbert's "The Police Bullies"

CARL: So if you think about Bob Herbert and the way he started, how might you start this as you write it?

WILLIAM: Thirteen-year-old Daryl Jones was fighting with his uncle . . .

CARL: That's a good start, you've really got the sound of this kind of writing.

WILLIAM: Thirteen-year-old Daryl Jones was fighting with his uncle . . . over the sink . . .

CARL: What might you write next? Do you want to tell more of the story, or do you want to use a quote?

WILLIAM: Quote. That's what he [Bob Herbert] uses.

CARL: So what quote would you use?

WILLIAM: [skims his interview notes] Maybe this part. "I wanted to use it, and he wanted to use it, so we had an argument," he said.

CARL: So I'd want you to start writing this story now. Try out what Bob Herbert did, that summary, quote, summary, quote rhythm. Are you ready to try that?

WILLIAM: Yeah.

Just before the share session, Ms. Lee and I asked William to show us what he had written after the conference (see Figure 2–10). We saw that he had taken what he had learned from looking at Bob Herbert's piece and used it successfully to write the story of Daryl's argument with his uncle.

When I'm making a teaching decision, I draw upon my knowledge of good writing by asking myself, "What do I know about good writing that makes sense to teach this student?" This question helps me recall what I know about the qualities of good writing, as well as the kind of text a student is making, and then I look at the student's writing with that knowledge as my lens. In my conference with William, I knew that the stories editorialists tell to support their point of view often mix narration and quotation. Since William had the raw materials to make these stories but didn't know how to put them together into a text, the goal of my teaching was to help him get an image of how this kind of text goes.

The question "What do I know about the writing process that can help this student?" helps me draw upon all I know about the strategies writers use to make a piece of writing, from finding an idea to editing the final draft. Often I'll put myself in the student's shoes and think about what I would do if I were trying to do the same kind of work. Or I'll remember a strategy I saw another student use, or a strategy a published writer I've read about relies on. In my conference with William,

> Another person who dislikes this saying is Daryl Jones. He had to wash dishes in the sink but his uncle wanted to use the sink too. Daryl and his uncle argued with eachother until Daryl's father came in and broke it up.
>
> During the argument, Daryl's uncle used the phrase "That's life."
>
> "I felt bad after the fight because I disobeyed my mom, she always told me to respect my elders and I didn't do that," Daryl said. "I was really mad at my uncle because he thought he could control me."
>
> His uncle thought that since he was older than Daryl, he could take advantage of him and he used the saying as a defense.

FIGURE 2-10   William's revision work

I had him take a look at Bob Herbert's editorial not only because I wanted him to get an image of how he could craft his stories, but also because writers study other writers' text in the process of making their own.

As I make my decision, I also consider the question "What do I know about this student as a writer?" I recall what I already know about the student, and I keep in mind what I've learned so far in the conference. What I choose to teach a student about good writing or the writing process should lie within what socio-psycholinguist Lev Vygotsky (1962) called a learner's "zone of proximal development." That is, I want to give the student a challenge he can meet now *with my assistance* that later he'll be able to do on his own. In my conference with William the week before, I learned he could tell a story using several sophisticated craft techniques. I felt that with my help, he could write his stories in the style of a *New York Times* editorialist and add what he learned to his repertoire of craft techniques.

Finally, I ask the question "What do I know about how children grow and develop as writers?" I remember what I've read about the developmental stages that children go through as they learn to write, and what I've learned about the kinds of writers who typically populate the grade in the school I am currently teaching. For example, I know, from reading Don Graves' (1994) summary of the research on children's growth as revisors of their writing (232–34), that it makes sense to teach most kindergarten or first-grade students about revision by nudging them first to add on to the end of their pieces. William immediately reminded me of some of the sophisticated writers I had in my classes when I taught eighth grade. What I had learned about the growth and development of those students years earlier helped me decide what I should teach William on this day.

Over time, I've found that making teaching decisions in many conferences has become easier. And quicker, too—rarely do I have "Hamlet" conferences in which I agonize for several minutes over the decision. That's because every time I'm happy with a conference and its results, that conference and what I taught the student in it becomes part of my repertoire of successful conferences. Then, when I confer about the same issue with another student who has similar writing experience and abilities, I can teach the same strategy or technique to that student. With experience, making teaching decisions becomes intuitive.

It also became easier to make teaching decisions once I realized that a conference isn't the search for the Holy Grail, the one perfect thing to teach a child. There are often several worthwhile things to teach students, and whichever one we pick will help them. We could teach a child who is having trouble coming up with an idea how to freewrite, how to look around the room and let objects and people spark ideas, or we could teach her to reread entries in her writers notebook or finished pieces in her folder and let this writing lead her to new ideas. No matter which one of these strategies we pick, it will probably help the student find an idea.

The Teacher's Role in the Second Part of the Writing Conference

It was a long way down to the bottom of Whiteface Mountain, the highest peak at the Lake Placid ski resort that had hosted the 1980 Winter Olympics. I had never tried to ski a mountain this advanced before, preferring instead the gentler slopes much further down the mountain. Over lunch, however, my friend Artie Voigt had convinced me to ride the lift with him to the top. "I've been watching you," he assured me, "and I know you're ready for the big ride."

But when the lift dropped us on the top of Whiteface, I felt like a sure candidate for one of those "Great Falls in Skiing History" videos. Artie noticed my fear, and chuckled. As he snapped his ski boots onto his skis, he said, "You can do this. Just don't look at the whole mountain. Take it slope by slope."

"Yeah, right," I responded. I was wondering how embarrassed I would be if I took the ski lift back down the mountain.

"We'll do this together," Artie said. "I'll go down the first slope and stop. Follow in my tracks. Just do what I do." He pushed off, zigzagged down the slope for a minute, then stopped and raised his ski pole, beckoning me to follow.

I set my skis in the grooves that Artie's had cut into the snow, cursed under my breath, and pushed off down the mountain. I kept my eyes glued to Artie's path. Where he had zigged, I zigged. Where he had zagged, I zagged. And where he had stopped, I stopped. But before I could catch my breath, Artie was off again.

I played catch-up several more times, until finally Artie waved me past him. I zoomed down the rest of the mountain by myself, cutting my own grooves in the fresh mountain snow all the way to the bottom. When Artie arrived a few moments later, it was me who suggested that we take on Whiteface again.

When I work with teachers, I tell the story of conquering Whiteface Mountain because it's a good metaphor for how we help students become better writers in conferences. Artie, after all, was such a good teacher that winter afternoon. His good teaching began at lunch, when he told me he had been sizing me up as a skier, and that he thought I was ready to ski more advanced slopes. When the ski lift dropped us on the top of Whiteface, Artie didn't send me down the slope my own. He told me a strategy I could use to navigate the mountain, and then he guided me partway down the mountain, until he saw I was ready to go it alone. The strategy for getting down a mountain that Artie taught me that day helped me get down Whiteface in one piece, *and* it's a strategy I've used to get down every big slope I've skied since. With Artie's help, I became a better skier.

It's in the second part of a writing conference that we have a conversation with a student about how he can be a better writer. That is, we teach a student about writing work he then tries in his current piece of writing—*and that we hope he will use in future pieces of writing, too.* In my conference with Becky, for example, I taught her how to revise by contrasting the picture in her mind of what she was writing about to what she actually had on her paper—a strategy I hoped she would continue to use in the future. And in my conference with Nick, I taught him about how to set up the big idea of a piece in his lead—work that, again, I hoped he would do when he worked on subsequent pieces.

It's important I be crystal clear that our job in the second part of a conference *isn't* to try to fix up all that's wrong with a student's piece. Because I'm a more experienced writer than the students I teach, it wouldn't be hard for me to read their pieces and tell them what changes they should make. If this were the way I conferred with students, then I would be teaching them to be dependent on me to tell them what their writing needs. I wouldn't be teaching them to have the intentions and strategies they need to write well in the future *independent of me.*

We lead the conversation during the second part of the conference. As the conversational leader, we have several responsibilities. First, we give critical feedback to students about their writing work. Second, we teach students how to do their writing work better. Then in many conferences we nudge students to have-a-go. That is, we have students briefly try out what we've taught them with our assistance. And fourth, we link the conference to the student's ongoing work by setting an expectation that students will follow through after the conference.

In the first part of my conference with Becky, I had gotten on a line of thinking about her revision work and had decided to teach her a strategy to help her add detail to her sleepover story. I began the second part of the conference by giving her critical feedback about her work.

CARL: Becky, I'm really impressed that you made two revisions to your piece. I want to talk to you about how you can revise even better. Remember when I showed you my piece about my two cats? Remember how I stretched "My cats were sitting on the windowsill" by writing, "They were sitting so still, they looked like statues. Only their tails moved." Would you have been able to see what my cats looked like if I had just said, "My cats were sitting on the windowsill. *They looked good*"?

BECKY: [shakes her head]

CARL: I didn't give you much there, did I?

BECKY: No.

CARL: Becky, when you wrote, "We made popcorn. It was good," I have no idea of what you mean by "good."

BECKY: So I should just erase that?

CARL: [I chuckle.] No, no . . .

After giving Becky feedback, I was ready to teach.

CARL: What I'm going to do is help you to add on in a way that will help us understand what you mean by "good" when we read your piece. One thing that writers do when they're revising a piece is try to get a picture of what they're writing about in their heads. When I do this, and I can really "see" what I'm writing about in my mind, that helps me think of details I can add to my piece.

I taught Becky by giving her a short explanation of the strategy I wanted her to try. Then, because this was a new strategy for her, I nudged Becky to have-a-go with it by talking her through using it.

CARL: I'm going to have you try that. Which of these parts—the popcorn or the pizza—do you want to work on some more?
BECKY: The popcorn.
CARL: So can you see that popcorn in your head?
BECKY: Well, most of the time when I'm writing I actually get it onto the piece better than I talk.
CARL: I want you to talk it out right now, practice it before you write it. Talk about that popcorn.
BECKY: Well, it's like fresh popcorn, I just got it from the store, my dad just got it from the store . . .
CARL: Fresh popcorn from the store . . . and . . .
BECKY: And . . . and it's only one type of popcorn . . . it was plain . . .
CARL: You're saying so much more than just, "It was good."? [I say back to Becky what I heard her say about making popcorn.] *You made popcorn without butter. It was the plain popcorn fresh from the store.* When you said all that, I had a better sense of what you meant by "It was good."

The work that remained for me in the conference was to link what Becky and I had just talked about to her ongoing work in the workshop.

BECKY: So I could add that to my story?
CARL: That's a great idea. You could also look at the other place where you added on and see if you could write more than "It was good" in the same way that you did with me.
BECKY: Okay.
CARL: You're working really hard, Becky. You're doing something writers do when they revise—they really try to help us get a picture of what they're writing about. I'll check back later in the period to see how you make out with this work.

In this final part of our conversation, Becky was the one who actually linked what we had talked about to the work she would be doing after the conference. I responded by suggesting she see the strategy as something she might use across her piece, not just in the one section we had talked about. Finally, by telling Becky I would come back later in that period, I made it clear that I expected her to follow through with the work we had discussed in the conference.

Give Students Critical Feedback

We give students critical feedback about their writing work to create a context for our teaching. By "critical" I mean giving an honest assessment. When we point out what we've noticed about how students are doing their writing work, we give them information about what they need to do to become better writers—and we set up the teaching that follows.

We also give students feedback because many students will be more open to our teaching after they hear it. When we teach, after all, we are intervening in what students are doing. While some children welcome our teaching, others, quite honestly, do not. When I first wrestled with this reality, it didn't help matters that I was teaching adolescents, many of whom commit their life energy to resisting any and all adult interventions in their lives. I found that many of my students were less resistant to my teaching after I gave them feedback—that is, after I gave them a rationale for the teaching that would follow.

Whenever possible, we begin giving critical feedback by pointing out some of our students' strengths as writers, as I did in my conference with Becky:

CARL: Becky, I'm really impressed that you made two revisions to your piece. I want to talk to you about how you can revise even better.

Usually, I point out students' strengths that I intend to build on during the conference. Pointing out students' strengths like this helps shore up their confidence so they are more open to the feedback that follows about what they need to do to make their writing work better.

We can give students our assessment of their writing work in several ways. We might say what we've noticed directly, as I did in my conference with Nick when I realized he wasn't setting up his character's problem in the beginning of his short story:

CARL: You know, when I read what you've written so far, I don't really get a sense this is going to be a story about a boy who has trouble with his friends. From what you've written, my sense of the story is that it's about a boy dealing with his mom's illness.

We can also frame our feedback in the form of a question, and get confirmation from the student that our assessment of him is on the mark, as I did in my conference with William when I thought he didn't know how to put his interview notes together into a story:

CARL: William, I get the sense that you aren't exactly sure how you can turn your notes into stories. Am I right?
WILLIAM: I guess.

We can also give students feedback by comparing their work to the writing of authors the class has studied—ourselves, student writers whose work we have highlighted, or published authors such as Bill Martin, Jr. or Gary Soto—as I did in my conference with Doran in Chapter 1. When I explained to Doran that there was more to writing a lead than he realized, I reminded him of the feature article by Candace Purdom his class had read:

CARL: Let me tell you what I'm hearing here. In the lead of a feature article, there's that one sentence that's the heart of the whole article, where a writer tells her reader her angle on her subject, and you really have a feel for that sentence there. I want to talk about one other thing you could do. One thing I noticed about the bully article is Candace Purdom does more in her lead than what you're planning to do. The sentence you've got planned is like the one she has right here [I point to last sentence of the lead] where she goes, "Here are tips on making a tough spot easier."

Some teachers have reacted with discomfort when they hear me give students critical feedback. "Aren't you worried that you're going to hurt a student's feelings?" they ask me. I tell them I think it's essential that students get honest feedback about what they need to learn to be good writers. When we are up-front with our students from the beginning, and we tell them that in writing workshop we're going to give them critical feedback about their writing work, then students expect that's going to happen in conferences—and there's much less chance that there will be hurt feelings. I also tell teachers that in many conferences students are aware that something isn't working in their writing, and they are relieved when we name it for them and offer our help.

Teach Students

Once we've given students feedback, we teach. We teach students *one* technique or *one* strategy or *one* concept. We resist the temptation to teach several things—even though most of our students have many needs as writers—because we don't want them to be overwhelmed by our teaching, and because we don't want our conferences to get so long that we can only see one or two students during the workshop.

I've noticed that teachers who confer well have a repertoire of different ways of teaching students. In some conferences, these teachers teach by giving students an explanation. In others, they teach by referring a student to a writing mentor. And sometimes they teach by reminding students of what they talked about in mini-lessons. Before we can teach students, then, we must decide *how* we're going to teach.

Give Students an Explanation   We can teach by giving a student a concise explanation of how writers do the work we're talking about. In my conference with Becky, for example, I gave her an explanation of a strategy for adding detail to her piece:

CARL: One thing that writers do when they're revising a piece is try to get a picture of what they're writing about in their heads. When I do this, and I can really "see" what I'm writing about in my mind, that helps me think of details I can add to my piece.

I usually preface my explanation by saying that what I'm about to teach is something that writers do. There are several ways that I say this:

- "One thing I do when I'm [revising] is . . ."
- "I've noticed that when Tamara [a student in the class] is [revising], she . . ."
- "Something I know that Eloise Greenfield [or any other writer I know something about] does when she [revises] is . . ."
- "One thing that writers do when they're [revising] is . . ."

I find that telling students I'm teaching them something that writers do gives the explanation that follows an aura of importance. Implicitly, I am inviting students to become a member of the group of literate people whom Frank Smith (1988) calls the "literacy club" (9–11). And if the writer I refer to is someone students admire, then students are often motivated to try out what I teach them.

Connect Students to a Writing Mentor   Another way we can teach is to connect a student to a writing mentor that he can learn from during—and after—the conference. By "writing mentor" I mean another writer who is better at the writing work that the student and I are talking about in the conference. This writer might be one with much more experience, usually a published writer that we've studied in class. Or it might be a writer with comparable experience, such as a classmate who is particularly good at the work the student and I are talking about.

When we connect a student to a published author, we can explain what that author did in his piece that we'd like the student to try. In my conference with Nick, for example, I connected him to two writing mentors:

CARL: Nick, what I want to talk with you about today is how many short story writers set up the main character's problem right at the beginning of a story. Remember how in the first paragraph of "Spaghetti" [by Cynthia Rylant] you found out that Gabriel wishes for some company? Remember how in the first *sentence* of "The New Kid" [by Dori Butler] you find out Kayla hated being the new kid in school?

When we connect a student to a published author, we can also have the student study the piece and notice independently how the writer did what the student is trying to do. The student can study the piece during or after the conference. In my conference with William, I asked him to study the first section of Bob Herbert's "The Police Bullies" and notice how Herbert constructs stories out of his interview notes:

CARL: One thing you can do is read the stories that Bob Herbert tells in this piece and notice how he put them together. Could you tell me what you notice about that first section?

WILLIAM: Well, he [Bob Herbert] tells part of the story, and then Francisco tells part of the story . . . he [Herbert] uses quotes that he took from interviews.

CARL: Anything else you notice about the way it's put together?

WILLIAM: Detail. [he reads aloud] "[H]e was riding his bicycle home from work, and an unmarked car cut him off on Linden Boulevard in Queens."

CARL: So you're noticing how much information you get in a sentence. So it seems like your sentences will also need to be jam-packed with detail. You learn a lot about the story in just four, five paragraphs. So those are some things that could guide you as you write.

In Chapter 4, I include an in-depth discussion of how we can connect students to writing mentors in conferences.

A student's classmates can also be writing mentors. We can tell a student about one of his classmates who is doing the same kind of work in her writing—only she's really got the hang of it—and suggest that he go and talk with her about what she's doing. We might say, "Anayra, Pamela is doing some great work with writing dialogue in her memoir. I'd like you to ask her for a peer conference, and ask her to show you how she's doing this."

Remind Students of a Mini-Lesson   We can also teach a child by reminding him about a recent mini-lesson (or series of mini-lessons on the same topic), and suggest he try in his writing what we talked about with the whole class. One of the reasons we teach mini-lessons, after all, is to save us time when we confer. When we've explained a kind of writing work in a mini-lesson, we shouldn't have to repeat everything we said in every conference that focuses on that kind of work.

Let's say we're conferring with a child who is editing, and we've noticed she is reading her piece silently to herself—and missing errors we know she shouldn't be missing. We might teach her by referring to a mini-lesson we gave on self-editing.

CARL: Remember that in yesterday's mini-lesson we talked about how when writers edit their pieces, they often read them aloud? And how we talked about how reading our writing out loud helps us focus on every word and see mistakes we might have missed if we read it silently?
TANYA: Yeah.
CARL: That's what I'd like you to try.

Of course, it isn't enough to remind some students about a mini-lesson. Even when we gave an especially clear and brilliant mini-lesson just fifteen minutes earlier, a student may need to hear us give the same explanation again. Sometimes, too, when we ask a student, "Remember in yesterday's mini-lesson how we talked about . . . ?" he replies, "No," or, "I didn't really get that."

Nudge Students to Have-A-Go
In many conferences, we nudge students to have-a-go—that is, to try out what we've just taught them *during the conference*. During the have-a-go, we support their initial attempt at doing the work we've just discussed. The have-a-go is an assisted performance—with our assis-

tance, students get a feel for how to do the work and are able to continue with it independently once the conference is over. In his article "Transactional Heat and Light: More Explicit Literacy Learning" (1998), Randy Bomer explains that in this part of the conference, we give students a chance to make sense of our teaching:

> In mini-lessons and conferences, I try to give students some experience at *doing* something, rather than just hearing about it. To be really teaching, to make sure the learner has an opportunity to construct understanding, I need to get the student actively constructing a new way of doing, a new practice in her repertoire. (14)

When I talk about the have-a-go with teachers, I ask them to remember how they learned to ride a bicycle. I tell them how my dad held on to the back of my bike during my initial attempts to ride, keeping me upright as I got the feel for riding. This was the have-a-go part of my dad's teaching. Eventually, of course, my dad let go—just like we let go at the end of a writing conference—and I wobbled down the street on my own, gaining more and more assurance with each driveway I passed.

When I nudge students to have-a-go, I usually have them talk through what they will write instead of having them do the actual writing. In my conference with Becky, we talked about how she could write more detail about the popcorn by using the strategy of seeing it in her mind.

CARL: I'm going to have you try that. Which of these parts—the popcorn or the pizza—do you want to work on some more?

BECKY: The popcorn.

CARL: So can you see that popcorn in your head?

BECKY: Well, most of the time when I'm writing I actually get it onto the piece better than I talk.

CARL: I want you to talk it out right now, practice it before you write it. Talk about that popcorn.

BECKY: Well, it's like fresh popcorn, I just got it from the store, my dad just got it from the store . . .

CARL: Fresh popcorn from the store . . . and . . .

BECKY: And . . . and it's only one type of popcorn . . . it was plain . . .

CARL: You're saying so much more than just, "It was good" [I say back to Becky what I heard her say about making popcorn.] *You made popcorn without butter. It was the plain popcorn fresh from the store.*

When you said all that, I had a better sense of what you meant by
"It was good."

During the have-a-go, I want students to make the necessary decisions about their writing. In my conference with Becky, I asked her
which part she wanted to work on further. It's important to keep in
mind that in an assisted performance, it's the student's performance that
we're assisting. If we make the decisions, then the have-a-go becomes
our performance, not the child's. (In some conferences, of course, students will say "I don't know" when we ask them which part they want
to work on. In these conferences, I will go ahead and select a part for
them to try the work we've been discussing.)

To nudge a student to talk out his writing, I ask him open-ended
questions. In my conference with Becky, I asked her, "So can you see
making that popcorn in your head?" When I asked Nick to imagine how
he could set up the problem in the lead of his short story, I said, "How
do you think you could do that?" Open-ended questions like these put
the responsibility for the writing on the student.

This is another juncture in the conference where we need to be
wary of asking leading questions. Imagine that instead of asking "So can
you see that popcorn in your head?" I had asked Becky, "Was the popcorn good because you enjoyed passing the bowl around with your
friends?" This question might have led Becky to add on a part about
how passing the popcorn around made her feel close to her friends—a
meaning that I would have led her to, not one that she arrived at on her
own. When we ask these kinds of specific questions, we also take the responsibility for generating new content and meaning away from students. What, then, would Becky have been able to do after the
conference when I wasn't there to ask her questions about another part
she wanted to revise in this piece, and in future pieces?

The have-a-go is a *brief* try. In many of my conferences, the have-
a-go lasts from one to three minutes. The point of the have-a-go, after
all, isn't for the student to complete the work we've discussed, but to
get a feel for how to do the work so he can do most of it on his own.
With Becky, for example, I helped her with one part of the piece, and
suggested she work on another herself. It also shouldn't be our goal in
the have-a-go that students master the work we've discussed with them.
Just like I wobbled on my bicycle after my dad let go, our students will
wobble as they do the work we've discussed after the conference. It's
over time, as they practice this work independently, that they become
better at doing it.

The have-a-go gives us an opportunity to assess our teaching. Sometimes during the have-a-go we realize what we've decided to teach a student is out of his zone of proximal development. In a conference with a first grader, we might realize that it was a mistake to try to teach him to add-on to the middle of his story, and that instead we should help him with adding more to the end. And sometimes when a student has trouble during the have-a-go, we realize we need to teach him in a different way, perhaps by referring him to a piece of literature or by showing him what one of his classmates did.

The have-a-go is part of most, but not all, conferences. We will nudge a student to have-a-go, for example, when we feel the student needs our support to succeed. This was the case in my conference with Becky. Or we'll include a have-a-go when what we're teaching a student is something we've only just begun talking about in mini-lessons—or if we haven't yet talked about the work with the whole class. With Becky, I thought it was essential that I give her some support, since her teacher hadn't yet talked about how writers picture what they're writing about to help them revise. We might choose *not* to include a have-a-go in a conference if we've just asked the student (and his classmates) to try the strategy we're teaching as part of a recent mini-lesson.

Link the Conference to Students' Ongoing Work

At the end of conferences, it's important that we let students know we expect them to do the work we taught them *right away*. Students, after all, don't learn how to do what we've taught them until they spend time trying it in their writing. The success of conferences, then, has everything to do with whether or not students use the time afterwards to do the work we talked about with them.

Teachers sometimes ask me if we're taking control over students' writing when we require them to try what we talk about with them in conferences. In response, I say we're taking control over their *time,* not their writing. The ultimate measure of a successful conference isn't really that a child does what we've asked her to do in that conference. Rather, it's that on her own, a couple of days later, a couple of weeks or months later, she decides to do the work we taught her to do again. That's not going to happen, however, unless she learns how to do that work, and for that to happen, we must expect that students will try out what we teach them.

I let students know I expect them to try out what we've talked about in several ways. In many conferences, I ask students, "What are you going to do now?" or say to them, "Tell me what your plans for your writing are now." In response, students describe how they're going to use what we talked about in their writing. Once the school year is under way and they've been in several conferences, students tell me how they're going to use what I taught them without my prompting. For example, after I had him have-a-go with the lead for his feature article, Doran said he wanted to incorporate what we talked about into his writing.

> DORAN: Yeah. If I was going to take after that, I could say, "So you want to get a toy that's very expensive. But you don't have so much money. Here are . . ." I could enlarge on that, like she did there.

In other conferences, I tell students exactly what I want them to do after the conference is over. In my conference with Nick, for example, I said, "Wow, if you start that way, it really sets Timmy's problem up well. So try that. Skip a line and freewrite some of that right now. Go for it."

I've noticed some teachers are hesitant about giving students explicit instructions. They use phrases such as, "I'd like for you to . . ." or "Could you try . . ." Although these teachers do in fact want their students to follow through with what they taught them, these kinds of phrases can give students the impression they don't have to try the work discussed in conferences.

I've found some students take conferences more seriously when I write down what I want them to do after the conference on Post-it notes. I ask them to stick the Post-it in their writers notebooks, or on their drafts. At the end of some conferences, instead of using a Post-it, I ask students to make an "assignment box" in their notebooks or on their drafts in which they write what they are supposed to do after a conference.

I often end conferences by telling students that I'll be back to see how the work we talked about goes. The last thing I said to Becky, for example, was "I'll check back later in the period to see how you make out with this work." Twenty minutes later, I dropped by her table for a minute to take a look at the work she had done. I follow through with other students at the end of the period, during the transition from writing time to the share session. As students are gathering on the rug, I ask them to show me their work. I may glance at their work right then, or I might hold on to it to glance at later during the day, or that evening.

Finally, I sometimes stick around for a few moments after I've ended the conference. I use the time to record my notes about the conference on my record-keeping form. I stay until a student has written a few words down—just enough to see he's on his way.

It's no secret, of course, that some students don't follow through with the work we talk about with them in conferences. When this happens, I ask them why they didn't follow through.

Some students don't follow through because they didn't understand what I taught them. I have another conference with these students and try to find a way to help them understand.

I've found that some students—especially those in the primary grades—have trouble remembering the work we did together in the conference after I've moved on to another student. Once I've learned this about a student, I try to match him up with a writing partner (usually a student who sits at his table). At the end of a conference, then, I'll suggest that he tell his partner the work he's going to do. Retelling the conference has helped many students carry it over into their independent work. And once a student has told a partner what he's going to do, should he have trouble remembering a few minutes later, he can ask his partner to remind him of what he said he was going to do.

And, of course, some students don't follow through because they simply don't feel like it. We *must* make it very clear from the first day of writing workshop that this is unacceptable. And there have to be real consequences for not following through, just as there are for students who don't do their math homework. Some teachers in the Teachers College Reading and Writing Project community, for example, keep students in from recess to work on their writing if they haven't followed through after conferences. When I was a classroom teacher, I used to make a note in my grade book when my middle school students didn't follow through. Students who didn't take conferences seriously received lower grades than those who did.

Post-Conference Work

After conferences are over, we still have work to do. This work will help us teach students in future conferences. And it will help us make decisions about what to teach our classes in mini-lessons.

Right after a conference, I take some notes about the conversation on the record-keeping forms I've attached to a clipboard I carry around with me. I jot down the date of the conference, what I learned about the work the student was doing, and what I taught him. Keeping records helps me remember what I talk about with students. And, when I review the notes I've taken from several conferences, I'm able to assess where I've taken each student so far as a writer, and where I still need to take him when I confer with him again. As the year progresses, my notes help me enter into conferences with lines of thinking in mind about each student as a writer that have grown out of all the conferences we've had before. (For a more in-depth discussion of record-keeping, see Chapter 6.)

I also try to check in with students sometime later in the period. Not only do these check-ins allow me to see if students are following through, they give me a chance to assess how students are doing with what I taught them. There are several ways to check in with students:

- Drop by their seats between conferences.
- Ask students to raise their hands and let us know once they've tried what we taught them.
- Ask students to show us their work as they gather on the rug for the share session.
- During the share session, ask students to show the class what they did.
- Ask students to give us their work after class so we can read it during our preps or after school.

Most check-ins are no more than a minute or two, just long enough for us to get a picture of what students did in response to our teaching. Occasionally, when I find that a student completely missed what we had talked about, I'll have another conference with him.

Finally, I take into account what I learned about students in that day's conferences as I plan for the next day's mini-lesson. Usually, I review the notes I took from that day's conferences to see if there were any issues that came up in several conferences. If I conferred with several first graders who weren't putting spaces between their words, then I might teach a mini-lesson the next day on some strategies for spacing. Or sometimes I decide the class would benefit from hearing about what I discussed in one conference that day.

Do We Get Behind Students' Agendas in Every Conference?

When I first started conferring, I was so thrilled a student was able to describe *any* kind of writing work that I immediately decided to get behind it, no matter that there was more important work I could be teaching him to do. For example, if a student told me that he was working on trying to figure out a great title for his story, I would help him with that, even though I knew he hadn't revised or edited his draft and needed to learn about both of these kinds of writing work.

Today, I don't get behind the work a child is doing in every conference. There are times when I ask a child to set another agenda for our conference, or even when I set the agenda, as I do in the following conference.

It was after lunch in Helene Lepselter's fifth-grade classroom in Chatterton School in Merrick, Long Island. For the past several weeks, the students had been studying the genre of feature articles. They had read many feature articles and had been gathering information in their writers notebooks about the topics they hoped to explore in their own articles. Today many of the students were beginning first drafts, and the students' expressions revealed a combination of excitement and anxiety. Mrs. Lepselter and I knelt down next to Chris, who was planning on writing his article on baseball.

CARL: What's the writing work you're doing right now?
CHRIS: Well, I'm writing about baseball. I'm going to write my lead.
CARL: Do you have a plan for your article?
CHRIS: Yeah. [He opens up his writers notebook to where he had written his plan. See Figure 2–11.]
CARL: [I look at the plan.] So it sounds to me like you have a structure in mind for your article. So in your lead you're going to talk about how baseball is one of the best sports and how there are baseball legends, then you want to have a part about baseball facts, like who invented baseball and who Ty Cobb was, and finally you want to have a part where you talk about tips for playing baseball.
CHRIS: Yeah.
CARL: I'm curious, Chris. What are you trying to say in this article?
CHRIS: I kind of want to write about the legends and facts and what you need to do to play baseball.
CARL: I'm not quite sure how Ty Cobb and how to play baseball fit together in the same piece.
CHRIS: Well . . . I'm not sure if I'm going to use Ty Cobb. I just put some ideas down.

I stopped and told Mrs. Lepselter that even though Chris wanted to begin writing his lead, I had decided not to get behind this agenda. While I was impressed that Chris knew that writers often plan out their drafts before they write them, and that feature articles have several different parts, I thought Chris needed to learn that feature articles are focused on a single big idea, and that all the parts of an article should work together to develop that big idea. In this conference, I was going to set the agenda for Chris's writing work.

FIGURE 2–11 Chris's plan for his feature article

I turned back to Chris, hoping to teach him how to make a plan for his article that would help him develop one big idea.

CARL: You know how we've been talking about how feature articles have an angle, one big idea that the whole piece is about? You've got several big ideas in your piece. Baseball legends could be a big idea for an article, what you need to play baseball could be another. So instead of helping you with writing your lead, I'm going to talk about how you can write your piece with just one big idea. [I pull a feature article out from under my clipboard.] Remember that in yesterday's mini-lesson Mrs. Lepselter talked about how in the feature articles your class has read—like this one about bullies [by Candace Purdom]—the authors set up their big ideas in their leads—like what to do if a bully is picking on you—and then each part of the articles are all about this big idea?

CHRIS: [nods]

CARL: So what's your angle about baseball going to be?

CHRIS: [thinks for a moment] How to play baseball.

CARL: What do you mean, "How to play baseball?"

CHRIS: Like what you need to do to play baseball, like how to catch a baseball, how to throw, how to field . . .

CARL: So the basics of playing baseball—catching , throwing . . .

CHRIS: Yeah.

CARL: You know, Chris, I want to tell you that before I start a draft, I often make several plans for the piece. I'd like you to try making another one, and this time, try to have all the parts fit your angle about how to play baseball. So in your lead you're going to say . . .

CHRIS: I'm going to say I'm writing about tips for playing baseball.

CARL: And just like in the bully article there are several sections after the lead, you'll need to imagine what your sections will be. What do you think you'll write about in your first section?

CHRIS: Hitting.

CARL: So, good, your first section fits with your angle. What could the other sections be?

CHRIS: Catching . . . throwing . . . pitching . . . maybe how to run the bases.

CARL: You seem to be on the right track, Chris. I'll check back later this period and see how your plan turns out.

When Mrs. Lepselter and I checked in with Chris later that period, we were pleased to see he had written a new plan for the article (Figure 2–12), and that he had started his first draft. We were impressed that both the plan and the draft focused on the skills players need to play baseball.

Sometimes teachers ask me if I have taken away a child's ownership of his writing process when I decide not to get behind the work he has told me he is doing. I answer, "Yes, I have." While I value ownership, I also value teaching, and sometimes these two values conflict. Each conference is such a precious teaching opportunity, and I want to be sure to use it to teach a child what I feel he most needs to learn at this point in time. For example, I believe that had I allowed Chris to own his original plan for his article, then I would not only have missed an opportunity to teach him something he needed to learn about writing well, I would have been shirking my responsibility as a writing teacher.

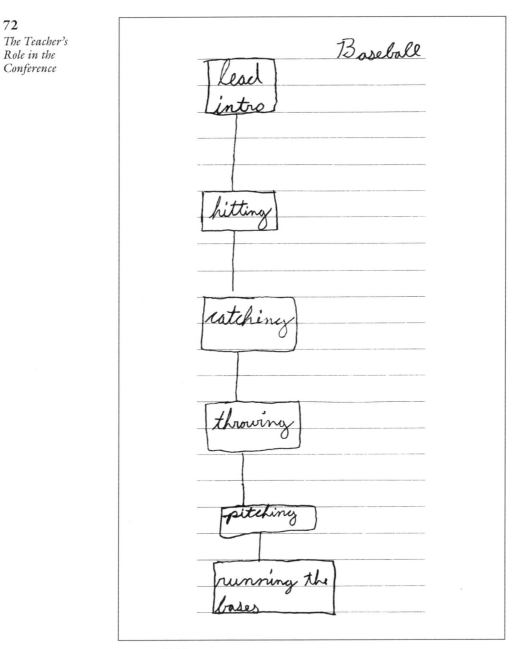

FIGURE 2–12   Chris's revised plan

I don't take this decision lightly. When I don't get behind a student's agenda, it's because of one or more of these reasons:

- There is work that he has already done that I could help him learn to do better.
- He left out a "step" in the writing process (e.g., he didn't make any revisions to his draft).
- There is another kind of work I know he needs to learn how to do at this stage in the writing process.
- He would benefit from trying out the writing work the class is studying in mini-lessons.

In my conference with Chris, I set the agenda because I felt he needed to learn something important about planning a piece of writing—that the plan grows out of the writer's focus. Thus, I nudged him to revisit the plan he had made for his article and rework it, instead of teaching him something about writing a lead.

Often, when I decide not to get behind a student's agenda, I ask him what other kinds of writing work he's doing or planning to do. Writers, after all, do many kinds of work in the process of rehearsing, drafting, revising, or editing a piece of writing. A student who tells us he is trying to figure out what his title should be may also be planning on rereading his draft to consider whether or not he should add more information. If we ask this writer, "What other work are you planning on doing?" he might say, "I'm going to add-on, too." Then we can still support his agenda *and* satisfy our need to use conferences to teach students about the writing work they need to learn most at that time.

What Do We Teach Students Who Are Done?

In many of our writing workshops, we confer with students who tell us they are "done." What, then, do we confer with them about? In the first part of a conference, after all, we talk with a student about the work she's *doing*. A student who is done isn't doing any work.

Sometimes we don't confer with students who tell us they are done *because they really are done*. In our zeal to teach students to be better writers, we sometimes forget that there comes a point when there's little to gain from nudging a second grader who has worked several days on a draft—or an eighth grader who has spent several weeks—to revise her piece one more time. If a child has worked for an appropriate amount of time on a piece, has brought it through every stage of the writing process, *and* has tried out what we talked with her about in previous conferences and what we've been talking with the class about in mini-lessons, then my response is a simple one. I congratulate her for all the hard work she's done, ask her what she's learned from writing the piece, and move on to the next conference.

Many students, however, tell us they're done as soon as they've finished their drafts. These students make few if any revisions and do little editing. It's these students especially who usually need our help to learn how to revise and edit.

When I confer with these students, I have a conversation with them about writing work they *could* do, and then I teach them something about that work. To get this conversation going, I take a look at the student's writing and then tell him what the piece tells me about his strengths as a writer, and what the piece tells me he needs to learn to grow as a writer.

I was working in Jackie Allen-Joseph's classroom at P.S. 261 in Brooklyn. As we walked together between the tables where her third and fourth graders were busy working, we noticed that Maya wasn't writing. Ms. Allen-Joseph was surprised, and explained to me that Maya had been excited by the mini-lessons she had given the last several days on how to develop a scene, and couldn't wait to get back to her memoir each day. With this in mind, we sat down next to Maya, and I began the conference.

CARL: So how's it going here with your work?

MAYA: I don't really know. I just did my first draft, so I guess I'm done.

CARL: So when you finish a draft, Maya, what's the work you usually do?

MAYA: Well, I think . . . I don't know.

CARL: Do you remember some of the work you did last year when you revised? What kinds of things did you do?

MAYA: I wasn't as good then as this year.

CARL: You're a more powerful writer this year?

MAYA: Yeah.

CARL: Maya, what do you think your piece needs to be a better piece of writing?

MAYA: [thinks for a moment] I don't know.

CARL: So you're not quite sure what you could do right now?

MAYA: Right.

At this point in the conference, I turned to Ms. Allen-Joseph. I pointed out that even though Maya had told us she was done, I still gave her plenty of opportunity to set a revision agenda, first by asking her about the kinds of revision work she had done on previous pieces, and then by asking her what she felt her memoir needed to be a better piece of writing. I explained how I prefer to get behind a child's agenda instead of imposing my own.

However, my questions didn't help Maya come up with any ideas for what she could do to revise her draft. To make a teaching decision, I explained, I would have to read Maya's draft and see what kind of revision work would make sense to teach her. I turned back to Maya and resumed the conference.

CARL: Can I take a look at your writing?

MAYA: [nods]

CARL: [I read Maya's piece. See Figure 2–13.] Maya, I'll tell you some things I noticed. First off, as I was reading this I felt like I was right there with you. You have a real knack for bringing us into a scene. Some of the sentences you wrote are marvelous, like your family clapping like cymbals. That helped me hear how the applause sounded.

MAYA: [beams]

CARL: I'm curious about this first part, why you stretched it out, and not these other parts—the scavenger hunt, the gifts, the sleeping routine, your mom tucking you in?

MAYA: I think it's because I usually do that. I take one idea and just stretch it out, and then take the other ideas, and just take those and detail them in certain ways that aren't too big, so it wouldn't be like this long thing.

I turned again to Ms. Allen-Joseph to share my thinking. I told her it was easy to see the footprints of her teaching in Maya's writing, particularly in how Maya developed the first scene in her memoir in which she blew out the candles on her birthday cake. What struck me as I read the rest of the piece was how each of the subsequent scenes—the scavenger hunt, her bedtime routine, her mom tucking her into bed—were just one sentence long. And it struck me, too, that Maya was afraid that developing more than one scene would make her piece too long. It made sense to me, I explained, to nudge Maya to try stretching another scene, both to practice what she had learned this past week, and to see that developing more than one scene could help her captivate her readers' interest even further.

CARL: Hmmm . . . I'm going to talk with you about stretching several scenes in a piece. In the memoirs your class has read, the writers stretched several scenes, not just one.

Birthday Wish

As I bent down to blow out the candles on my fancy birthday cake, I turned my head and could see the sun setting. I bent down to blow the flaming wax out. The kettle on my mom's stove interrupted me, but it was singing like the sweetest mockingbird in the country. My mom turned the knob on the stove to off, and the singing stopped. When I blew out the flames on my fancy cake, everyone started clapping. I hated it when when my family did that. The noise from their hands was like cymbals being smashed together. It was like I had just finished a performance and everyone was clapping wildly! My wish was the best part of my birthday. It was a wild wish, a crazy wish, and an awesome wish! Chop, Chop, went the slicer, I call it, slicing up pieces of delicious, fancy, chocolate cake with huge layers of chocolate frosting on top with enormous spoonfuls of sprinkles showered on my fancy cake. I took every bite very slowly to savor the moment of the rich chocolate in my mouth. Mmmmmmmm! Delicious! I had a scavenger hunt. Gifts were in very weird

FIGURE 2–13   First draft of Maya's "Birthday Wish"

places, but I got to them. I did my sleeping routine and crawled into my bed, like a crab scurrying back into the ocean! My mom tucked me in with her wonderful long arms, kissed me on the head and told me, "Dream the sweetest dream, birthday girl." What I wished for my birthday stays a clueless mystery. I love my wish, but I think I will keep it to myself for the time being.

FIGURE 2–13   *(Continued)*

MAYA: [nods]

CARL: You know, Maya, you're just like a lot of writers who write memoirs. Like Jean Little, for example. You know that story from *Little by Little,* the one in which her classmates make fun of her because of her eyeglasses?

MAYA: Yeah.

CARL: Both you and Jean Little packed several scenes into a single piece of writing. But Jean Little didn't just stretch the first scene and list the rest. She stretched most of the scenes, the scenes that really helped us understand what she went through. You could revise by trying to make your memoir more like the ones you've read in class so far this year. That's what I want you to try—picking one of these other scenes and stretching it like you stretched the birthday candles.

MAYA: Okay.

CARL: Which one would you want to try?

MAYA: Maybe . . . I kind of like it the way it is.

CARL: I can understand that. But I'm still going to challenge you to take a risk as a writer by trying out Jean Little's way of stretching several scenes. And if you decide you don't like what it does to your piece after trying it, that's okay. But when I visit your classroom, I nudge students to try things I think will help them grow

as writers. So which scene do you want to stretch—the scavenger
hunt, the sleeping routine, your mom tucking you in . . .

MAYA: I think . . . my mom tucking me in.

CARL: Good. I want you to get another piece of looseleaf paper and try
stretching that scene out now.

MAYA: Okay.

CARL: I'll check in with you later in the period to see how it goes.

When we checked in with Maya at the end of the period, she had
finished revising the tuck-in scene (see Figure 2–14). When I asked her
if she thought this revision made her memoir a better a piece of writing,
she nodded and said that "it was good because you can see this part
now, too." Ms. Allen-Joseph and I were glad we had nudged Maya to
try the revision, even though she was initially resistant to making it.
Maya had learned something about the value of revision—that when
she returned to a first draft and worked on it further she could indeed
improve it.

To me, the hardest thing about conferring with students who are
done is deciding what to teach them. I've found that how I read their
drafts has a lot to do with how good a decision I'll make. If I read simply looking for anything to teach them—which is how I handled these

My mom tucked me in with her wonderful long arms, kissed me on the head and told me, "Dream the sweetest dream, birthday girl." I loved it when my mom tucked me in. She was my best tucker-inner. She sang to me and rubbed my back to make me feel special and she was like my dreamkeeper. My mom made me dream special dreams that night.

FIGURE 2–14   Maya's revision work

conferences when I was new to conferring— then I'll probably make a poor decision. The first thing I noticed when I started reading Maya's draft, for example, was that she hadn't paragraphed. While it certainly wouldn't have been wrong to teach Maya about paragraphing, I think that the revision work I taught her how to do was more important for her to learn at this point. Paragraphing could wait until another conference.

To help me make a good teaching decision, then, I keep several questions in mind as I read their drafts.

- What do I know about what this student needs to grow as a writer? Does it make sense for me to teach him how to do this in this draft?
- What has the student done well in his draft? Does it make sense to have him do more of this work, to get practice with it?
- What have I taught in recent-mini-lessons? Does it make sense to have the student try out what I've taught in these mini-lessons in this draft?

Two of these questions helped me decide what to teach Maya. In the first minute of the conference, for example, I learned that Maya didn't have much of a sense of revision. Consequently, I read her piece looking for a way to teach her about revision. And as I read, I soon noticed how she had done a beautiful job with developing the first scene— and that since she hadn't developed any other scenes, it would make sense to have her practice this again.

It's predictable that in these conferences we will sometimes have to deal with students' reluctance to work more on their pieces. Maya, in fact, said what many, many students have said to me: "I kind of like it the way it is." What I said in response to her is what I have said to numerous other students. I remind them how in writing workshop, I want them to be the kind of writers who take risks and try new things in their writing. And I also give them an out: I tell them that if they don't like the results of the work I nudge them to try, they don't have to keep the changes they've made. The point of a conference, after all, is to help our students become better writers, not to fix up their drafts and make them better pieces. While I was pleased that Maya's revision work improved her piece, I was more pleased that she experimented with writing a part of her first draft in a different way. Even had she decided not to keep this revision, I would have considered this conference a successful one because Maya had gotten a feel for what writers do when they revise a draft.

WE LEARN TO confer well by concentrating on how to have good conversations with students about their writing. In both parts of the conference conversation, we have conversational responsibilities. In the first part, when we talk with a student about his writing work, we invite the student to set an agenda for the conference, and we get on a line of thinking about his writing work. In the second part, when we talk with a student about how to be a better writer, we give the student critical feedback, we teach, we may nudge the student to have-a-go, and we link the conference to the student's ongoing independent work.

In the midst of these conversations, we have crucial intellectual work to do. As we talk, we make an assessment of a student's writing work. And, with that assessment in mind, we decide what to teach the student in the conference.

The conference conversation is a complex and challenging one, and it doesn't become any less so once we understand our role in it. Knowing my role, however, has helped me approach conferences with a confidence I lacked during my first few years as a writing workshop teacher. Today, after I say "How's it going?" I know where I want the conversation to go, and how I can help it get there.

References
Bomer, Randy. 1998. "Transactional Heat and Light: More Explicit Literacy Learning." *Language Arts* 76 (1): 11–18.

Butler, Dorothy. 1995. "The New Kid." *Cricket* 22 (12): 54–56.

Graves, Donald. 1994. *A Fresh Look at Writing.* Portsmouth, NH: Heinemann.

Herbert, Bob. "The Police Bullies." 1997. *The New York Times.* March 7, A35.

Little, Jean. 1987. *Little by Little: A Writer's Education.* New York: Viking.

Purdom, Candace. 1994. "So a big, bad bully is coming after you . . ." *The Chicago Tribune, Kids News.* August 23, 1.

Rylant, Cynthia. 1985. "Spaghetti." In *Every Living Thing,* 31–33. New York: Bradbury.

Smith, Frank. 1988. *Joining the Literacy Club: Further Essays Into Education.* Portsmouth, NH: Heinemann.

Vygotsky, L. S. 1962. *Thought and Language.* Edited and translated by Eugenia Hanfmann and Gertrude Vakar. Cambridge, MA: MIT Press.

Teaching Students About Their Conference Role

3

I couldn't wait to confer with students when I launched my first writing workshop twelve years ago. I had just read Lucy Calkins' *The Art of Teaching Writing* (First Edition, 1986), and I was impatient to have the kind of in-depth conversations with my sixth graders that Calkins describes.

For my first conference, I sat down next to Syeda, one of my favorite students in the class. I took a deep breath and said, "How's it going?" just like Calkins suggests. Syeda wrote a few more words, then put her pen down and nervously shifted her gaze from her paper to my face. She said nothing. I waited a few moments, certain that Syeda just needed some time to gather her thoughts. Finally, I repeated the question and gave her paper a quick glance to make sure she knew I was asking about her writing.

Syeda opened her mouth and whispered slowly, "Okay."

"Okay," I reflected back. "I'm glad that it's going okay." Inside my head, though, I was thinking something else. *Okay? That's all she's going to say?* For a long, awkward moment, Syeda and I just looked at each other, until I stammered, "I'm really glad it's going okay." I stood up quickly and walked off, before Syeda could see my cheeks redden.

The other students I conferred with that day didn't say much more than Syeda. After a couple more conferences, I could no longer stand the long silences. I felt like I had to do *something,* so I gave up asking students how their writing was going. Instead, I started conferences by reading their drafts, and then I told them what I thought they should do to make their writing better. *Tunde, you should tell more in this part about how your sister bugs you. Aurora, you should start with some dialogue to make your beginning more interesting.* I knew from reading Calkins' book that I was taking control of my students' writing, but I felt I had no choice because they wouldn't—or couldn't—talk with me.

Many of the teachers I work with as a staff developer have expressed the same frustration with the passive role their students play in conferences. They ask me how to encourage students to take a more active role, to help them be like the students featured in the transcripts of conferences I've included in Chapters 1 and 2.

In response, I tell teachers there are reasons why students don't talk much in conferences, especially when we confer with them in September. When I think back to my first conferences, I understand why my students were so passive. None of my students had been in a writing workshop before—which meant, of course, that none of them had ever had a writing conference with a teacher. Syeda and her classmates were no doubt startled, if not highly apprehensive, when I knelt next to their desks and asked them how their writing was going. And since no one had ever conferred with them, they hadn't yet had a chance to learn how to talk about their writing with a teacher.

Since my first conference with Syeda, I've learned that students can learn to hold up their end of the conversation in conferences. They can learn to talk fluently and precisely about their writing at the beginning of conferences when they set the agenda for the conversations. And they can learn to do the same when they respond to our research questions and to our teaching once we've assumed the lead role in the conversation.

In very concrete and practical ways, we can teach students to take an active role in conferences:

- First, we need to immerse them in the conference conversation at every opportunity.
- Second, in mini-lessons, we can directly teach students about their role in conferences (see Figure 3–1).
- Third, we can use conversational strategies that support students' talk in conferences and teach them how to talk about their writing.

Immerse Students in the Conference Conversation

I've never met a child who doesn't already know how to have many different kinds of conversations. Children know how, for example, to negotiate with their parents for a later bedtime, or debate a classmate over which baseball league will win the annual All-Star game, or gossip with a friend about their classmates' crushes.

It follows, then, that children can learn how to have conversations with us about their writing. If we identify the conditions that enabled them to learn how to participate in various conversations, we can then make sure those conditions exist in our classrooms.

THE STUDENT'S ROLE IN A CONFERENCE

In the first part of the conversation:
- set the agenda for the conference by describing her writing work
- respond to her teacher's research questions by describing her writing work more deeply

In the second part of the conversation:
- listen carefully to her teacher's feedback and teaching
- ask questions to clarify and deepen her understanding of her teacher's feedback and teaching
- have-a-go with what her teacher taught her
- commit to trying what her teacher taught her after the conference

FIGURE 3–1   The student's role in a conference

From his research into how young children learn to talk, Brian Cambourne (1988) has identified these conditions (30–41). A child learns to talk, Cambourne says, because he is constantly immersed in conversation from the moment he is born. That is, through their own conversations with each other, the significant people in a young child's life demonstrate how talk goes, and its different purposes. And these same people engage the child in conversation, even before he can say a single word.

It's been my experience that students will begin to hold up their end of the conferring conversation a few weeks after we launch writing workshop. Like small children, our students will learn to do this if we constantly immerse them in the conference conversation and communicate the expectation that they will join us in these writer-to-writer talks.

Start Conferring on the First Day of Writing Workshop
As a staff developer, I launch writing workshops in classrooms all around the New York metropolitan area and around the United States. After my mini-lesson on the launch day, I move around the room and confer. As I talk with students, teachers listen in on the conversations.

As we debrief the launch afterwards, teachers sometimes question my eagerness to confer with students on that first day. They point out that several students seemed confused about why I was talking with them. They observe that some of them didn't have a whole lot to say about their writing. And those students who did talk, they say, had trouble explaining what they were doing in their writing. They wonder if they should wait a few weeks, until the children feel more comfortable with writing workshop and have a better sense of the writing process, before beginning their own conferences. That way, they think, the students will have something to say, and their conferences will go more smoothly.

I think it's absolutely essential to start conferring on the first day of writing workshop. Students learn to take an active role in conferences only if we expect them to, and if we give them frequent opportunities to practice talking like writers. By starting to confer on the day we launch our workshops, we let our students know that they are in a different kind of a classroom, one in which they will be required to talk with us about their writing. We may see only a few students on that first day, but most students notice that the teacher is talking with their classmates one-on-one. And when we confer on that first day, we begin to give students opportunities to practice talking about their writing, even if that practice means they say just a few halting words.

Imagine if we waited to talk with babies until after their first birthday. Most parents start talking with their children as soon as they are born. (Like many parents, I started talking to my daughter when she was still inside her mom.) This early talk is what prompts children to eventually start talking.

Go Out Into the Classroom to Confer

In earlier chapters, I've made a case for moving around the classroom to confer with students at their seats. Another benefit of going to students, instead of having them come to us, is that we immerse not only the child with whom we're conferring, but the children who sit nearby, too. Especially for students who are new to writing workshop, overhearing conferences like this helps children get more of a sense of how the conversation goes.

In many conferences, I am fully aware that several students are eavesdropping. I notice that one student has stopped writing and that another is leaning his body toward where I am conferring with his classmate. I usually allow the eavesdropping to happen, knowing that once I finish the conference, these Harriet the Spy wannabes will get back to work. I feel that what students learn about conferences by listening in makes up for the few minutes of writing time lost.

There are times when I actively encourage students to listen in on conferences. I may ask the children sitting around a table to give me their attention, and then I'll extend an invitation:

> Boys and girls, I'm sorry to interrupt your writing. I know some of you are unsure about what conferences are all about, so I'd like you to listen to the one I'm going to have with Gregory. Listening in might help you get a better sense of what happens in conferences.

In some classrooms, I've even stopped the entire class and had them gather around to listen to and watch a conference. After the conference is over, I talk with the students about what they just heard, and explain that the conferences I'll have with them will follow a similar pattern.

> I hope you noticed that in the first part of the conference, I asked Gregory what he was doing as a writer, and he told me he wanted to add some stuff to his first draft. When I confer with you, I'll ask you the same question, and I hope you'll tell me about the work you're doing. In the second part of

the conference, I taught Gregory a new way he could say more in his draft. When I confer with you, I'll also teach you something you can try that will help you become a better writer.

Since we want children to be able to listen in on conferences, we ought to give careful thought to how we seat them in the classroom. Putting students at individual desks in straight rows, for example, is the arrangement that makes it most difficult for students to hear conferences. Having them sit at tables, on the other hand, practically guarantees that they'll eavesdrop.

Demonstrate Writers' Talk in Mini-Lessons

One of the most effective ways to immerse students in writers' talk is to "talk the talk" ourselves in mini-lessons. When we teach students' writing discourse by using the words in context, we take advantage of children's prodigious ability to learn new words. Frank Smith's research has shown that the average child already knows ten thousand words at age four. By the time she finishes school, her vocabulary grows to at least fifty thousand words, just by hearing words used naturally and in context, and from reading them (1995, 42).

For example, when teaching students a strategy for getting started with a first draft, I might begin my mini-lesson with these words:

> I want to show you today how I got started with the first draft of my memoir about my father. In my writers notebook, I brainstormed a couple of possible leads. Then I picked the one that made me really want to write. Finally, I started writing off of it on a clean sheet of paper. I'll show you my work, so you can get a clear picture of what I did.

After a mini-lesson like this, many children do, in fact, immediately start using some of the words and terms they heard—"first draft," "memoir," "writers notebook," "brainstorm," "lead," and "write off." They pick up the words not because they're sponges, but because they need them to communicate clearly with us in conferences, with each other in peer conferences, and with the whole class in share sessions.

We mustn't be afraid that children somehow aren't "ready" to hear writers' talk. Even kindergarten and first-grade students are fully capable of learning words and terms writers use. I can't imagine that a gym teacher would introduce the game of basketball to children by saying, "What you do in this game is to take this round thing and bounce it up and down a lot and share it with your friends a couple of times until one of you thinks you can throw it into that metal circle." Of course, what the gym teacher would really say is, "What you do in this game is to dribble the basketball down the court, where you'll pass it to your teammates until one of you has a good shot at the basket." Students in this gym class—just like students in our workshops—learn these words because their teacher uses them in context, and because they need them to communicate.

Celebrate When Students Use Writers' Talk

One morning when my daughter was six months old, she opened her mouth and said, "Da-da-da-da-da-da." While I knew that she was just experimenting with consonant sounds—not addressing me—I was still thrilled. I immediately called out to my wife, Robin, and said, "Anzia is saying 'Da-da-da-da!'" (She, of course, came into the room and tried to get our daughter to say "Ma-ma-ma-ma.")

Millions of other parents are equally thrilled when the sounds that their babies make begin to approximate speech. They, too, celebrate those sounds by sharing the news with their families.

When our students begin to talk like writers, we should consider reacting with the same sense of joy. There are several ways that we can explicitly celebrate our students' use of writing discourse.

- After a conference, we might ask the class to stop writing so we can announce, "Class, I have to tell you about how Erika has just been talking like a writer. She just told me that she's 'putting a scene together by getting her characters to speak and by writing down their thoughts'." We could also celebrate a student's talk like this during a share session.
- During a share session, we might conduct a "symphony share" during which, one-by-one, students say out loud what they did as writers that period, trying especially hard to use the writing discourse they've learned.
- On a bulletin board, we can highlight examples of the ways students in the class are beginning to talk about their writing.

In all of these ways, we can show students how we value their use of writing discourse—and make it more likely they will use it when we confer with them.

Give Mini-Lessons That Help Students Understand Their Conference Role

I began the second day of a two-day workshop on conferring in Merrick, Long Island, by asking teachers how their conferences had changed since we had first met several weeks earlier. Trish Kelleher, a sixth-grade teacher at Chatterton School, reported that her students had begun to talk more in her conferences with them. When I asked her what she had done to cause this change, Trish replied, "We had a conversation about what they should do when I conferred with them."

There was a lot of wisdom in what Trish said that morning. When I began conferring years ago, I didn't ever think to have a discussion with my students about their role in conferences. While most students did eventually figure out what I expected of them, it took them several months. If only, like Trish, I had thought to have a conversation with my class about conferences, I could have saved myself a lot of frustration, and had better conferences, too.

As a staff developer, I've worked with teachers who have given mini-lessons about the role of teacher and student in conferences. The teachers have found that these lessons helped their students understand what they should say in conferences, and how to say it. What follows in this section are descriptions of three of these lessons.

Lead a Discussion About Conferences

Perhaps the simplest way for us to teach students about conferences is for us to initiate whole-class discussions about the subject. As students share their thoughts, we can assess their understanding of why we confer with them and the roles of teacher and student in the conversation. Then we know what to teach them.

Several months into the school year, Alexa Stott, then a first-grade teacher at P.S. 199 in Manhattan, was nudging her students to make the big shift from talking about what their stories were about to talking about the work they were doing as writers. Alexa figured that a whole-class discussion would help them understand what she was asking them to do, and why. She gathered her students together in their meeting area and began the discussion.

ALEXA: I want to talk with you about the conferences we have. I want you guys to talk to me about what you think conferences are, what they are for and what your job and my job is in a conference.

HALLE: I think conferences are for, like, if I was doing a piece of writing and you came over and you never knew what I was doing, then I would tell you a lot of things I was doing so you would know what I was doing.

ALEXA: Okay, Halle, what you are saying is that part of your role is to let me know about all of the work you have done. So, why?

HALLE: So, you write it down, so if it's good, sometimes you share it with the class.

EWEN: A conference is, well, if we aren't doing our work and then we see you coming, we don't know what to say, then you know that we weren't doing our work.

ALEXA: Interesting. Then, what are you saying my role is?

EWEN: To find out that we didn't do any work, that we were just playing around.

GABRIELLE: I don't think that, when we are doing conferences, it's about Ms. Stott finding out about if we are doing our work or not. I thought it was about finding out what we were *doing* in our writing.

At this point in the discussion, Alexa knew that some of the students in the class had noticed she wanted them to talk about the work they were doing as writers when she conferred with them. She also found out that students had different opinions about why she wanted this information. So Alexa pushed the class to speculate further about why she wanted them to talk about their writing work.

ALEXA: Okay, I think people are just throwing out their ideas about what conferences are for. So, if you think that conferences are about my finding out what work you are doing, why would that be important for me?

GABRIELLE: Well, I think that conferences are to help you with what you have to do.

ZOE: We found that when you have a conference . . . it helps me with my piece, more than by myself. Like with more strategies . . . you help so I have a way of doing it myself.

SAMANTHA: Ms. Stott is supposed to help us by giving us something we need to do.

GABRIELLE: To help us get better at doing stuff.

After this series of responses, Alexa felt that some of her students understood why she wanted them to talk about what they were doing as writers. Alexa chose to elaborate on these students' responses as a way of teaching the rest of her students about why she confers with them, and why she needed them to talk about their writing work.

ALEXA: So it feels like a part of all that you are saying is true. Our conferences are times for me to come around and help you individually. We may be working on stuff as a class, but each of us is different and has different needs as writers, so our conference time is time for us to work together to give you more tools as a writer.

GABRIELLE: Like what we *need* is maybe more than someone else.

ALEXA: Exactly. So, if I am coming around to help you as a writer, do I always need to hear about what your piece is about?

HALLE: No! You want to know how we are doing it. Like if we say we are doing the "building" structure [the class's name for a particular picture book structure] you want to know how we are doing that.

ALEXA: And why would that be more important?

GABRIELLE: Because you want to know what we are doing and what we are learning.

ALEXA: Okay, and because if you only tell me what this piece is about, it's hard for me to figure out how to help you with that piece. But if you tell me how you are trying out something, then I can help you to find strategies to use that will help you in all of your writing.

GABRIELLE: So, when you weren't there we wouldn't have to say, "Oh, I don't know what to do on this." We would know from a strategy that was already taught.

ALEXA: Exactly, so when I come over to you and ask, "What work are you doing as a writer?" I am more interested in helping you use strategies that will help your writing over lots and lots of pieces.

What's striking about Alexa's teaching is how carefully tailored it was to what students understood about conferences. One way, then, for the rest of us to provide equally tailored teaching is to ask our students what they think is going on when we're conferring with them.

Fishbowl Conferences in Front of the Class

Another way we can teach students about conferences is to "fishbowl" one of them in front of the whole class. That is, we confer with a child while the rest of the class observes and takes notes about what they notice the teacher and student doing in the conference.

When Holly Kim was a fifth-grade teacher at P.S. 321 in Brooklyn, she gathered her students together in the meeting area of her room for a fishbowl. She conferred with Melissa, who was planning to write entries in her writers notebook about her parents before starting a first draft of a memoir about them. Melissa was working on a list of memories about her parents in her notebook to help her think about which entries to write.

HOLLY: I'm going to have a conference with Melissa in front of all of you. I want you to try and notice as many things as you can about what happens in a writing conference. [turns to Melissa] So, Melissa, what's going on with your writing?

MELISSA: I'm writing off my list.

HOLLY: So you already have a seed idea and you made a list off of that idea. Now you're writing off of that list?

MELISSA: Yeah, I'm going to write a lot about my parents.

HOLLY: So how are you going to go about doing this?

MELISSA: I think I should add to my list and then write off of it.

HOLLY: So you're telling me that you want to add to your list and then write off of it. One of the things that good writers do when they're choosing a topic that seems pretty big is choose specific memories or moments about that person. For example, if you're writing about your best friend, you can't write about your whole friendship with her, but you can pick and choose the important moments that you've experienced with her. Then you write as much as you can about those important memories. So is your list a compilation of different memories that you have of them?

MELISSA: Yeah. There's a lot of things.

HOLLY: So now what you're doing is gathering all those things, but you still have to pick and choose what's important, right?

MELISSA: Yeah, I'm gonna pick, like Lessie Little does in "My Fella" [a piece in *Childtimes* in which Lessie Little shares several memories of her husband].

HOLLY: Oh, so you want to write a memoir that goes like "My Fella"?

MELISSA: Yeah, because she picked the most important things.

HOLLY: So after you develop your list, you're going to pick the most important things on that list, like Lessie Little does in "My Fella."

MELISSA: Yeah.

HOLLY: [shifts her gaze from Melissa back to the class] Okay, so what are some things you noticed in that conference?

EBONY: You asked Melissa how she was going to write more about her parents and you gave her advice on how to do it.

HOLLY: She's working on something. Her goal was to say more about her parents and I asked her how she was going to do that. I want to make sure that she has a strategy in her head. What else did I do?

LUIS: You were paraphrasing what she said.

HOLLY: Yeah, I was doing that a lot so she would know I was listening.

JEANNIE: You really wanted to know exactly what she was doing.

HOLLY: What was really great about this conference was that Melissa was prepared for it. She was prepared to talk to me. That's one of the things that you all have to be ready to do. When I sit with you, you have to be ready to tell me what it is that you're doing in your writing. Melissa did that. And not only did she tell me what she was doing, she told me what she's going to do to accomplish her goal, and why she chose that strategy. So when I sit with you, it's important that you're prepared to have a conversation with me. You have to be able to tell me exactly what you're working on in your writing and whether or not you're having a problem.

The discussion after the fishbowl gave Holly several opportunities to teach her class about the purpose of conferences, and the roles of teacher and student. Holly did this by elaborating on each of the students' responses, explaining why she did what she did ("I want to make sure she has a strategy in her head," "I was doing that a lot so she knew I was listening") and what she expected from them ("It's important that you're prepared to have a conversation with me").

After a fishbowl conference, we can ask students to practice the kind of talk they saw their classmate model. In a subsequent mini-lesson, Holly referred back to her conference with Melissa, reminding the class how Melissa had talked about her writing. Then she asked her students to practice talking about their plans for their writing that day, just like Melissa had done. First, they talked in twos or threes about their plans for the period. Then, one by one, they told the class what they were going to do. These are some of their responses:

SCOTT: I'm drafting, then I'm going to go to my revising.
STEPHEN: I'm seeing if I have any wrong spelling. Basically, I'm editing.
JEMEL: I'm trying to show the passage of time.
JENNY: Today, I'm going to write my next draft and really pay attention to my beginning and the middle.
BEN: I'm having trouble deciding on a good beginning, and I'm gonna be working on that.
RYAN: I'm doing a tally of what titles people think are best.
MALIKA: I'm picking a seed idea for my next piece.
JEFF: I'm taking Post-its and looking over my story to see where I can add more.

Some teachers have turned this kind of talk into a daily ritual in their workshops. At the end of a mini-lesson, they have students turn to their neighbors and say what their plans are for that day's workshop.

Not only does this kind of talk help students start their writing with more purpose, they're better prepared to have something to say in conferences. This ritual can take several other forms:

- When children return to their seats after a mini-lesson, they can write their plans for the period in a self-assignment box in their writers notebooks, or on a special sheet in their writing folder.
- Occasionally during the workshop, teachers can ask the students to stop their writing for a minute and talk with their neighbors about what they're doing as writers.
- During some share sessions, students can talk about what they're planning to do in their writing that evening, or during the next writing workshop period.

Coach Students During Fishbowl Conferences

Another way we can use fishbowl conferences to teach students their conference role is to coach students as we confer with them in front of the class. When we stop a fishbowl conference and nudge a student to talk about his writing work, for example, both the student with whom we are conferring and his classmates learn something about what to talk about in conferences.

Several months into the school year, Dana Hill, then a fifth-grade teacher at P.S. 37 in the Bronx, led her class in a study of how they could improve their talk about their writing work. As part of this study, Dana coached students in fishbowl conferences.

Dana felt that her coaching would be more successful if she could refer back to a conference that her class had already discussed. On the first day of the study, Dana gave the class a transcript of a conference she had had with Sammy, and the class had a discussion about how Sammy had talked about his writing. After the discussion, Dana put the class's noticings on a chart:

WHAT SAMMY DID	OUR NAME FOR IT
He started talking about his writing and his plans. He didn't wait for the teacher to drag it out of him. He jumped right in.	Having intentions and jumping into talking about them.
He used words that the class has been using—"many moments" piece.	Using our writing language.

WHAT SAMMY DID	OUR NAME FOR IT
Sammy was very involved in the conference. He told the teacher what he was going to do with the new information he learned.	Tell what you're going to do.
Sammy told the teacher where his idea came from. He compared his work to the writing of another author that the class has studied.	Give background information. Talk about the mentor for your writing.

On the second day of the study, Dana had a fishbowl conference with Henry. She was hoping to do some coaching in this conference, and just a few moments into the conversation—when Henry began to talk about the content of his piece instead of his writing work—she found that opportunity.

DANA: Can you tell me what you're doing as a writer today?

HENRY: I'm writing about going to the park and going to the zoo.

DANA: Okay, we're going to stop there. Let's think back to how Sammy jumped right into saying what he was doing. Sammy said, "I tried writing my story in different ways and I decided to make a 'many moments' piece." Does thinking about Sammy's talk give you ideas about how you might talk? Do you want to redo it?

HENRY: Yes.

DANA: Hi, Henry. Can you tell me what you're doing as a writer today?

HENRY: I wrote a draft . . .

DANA: Why don't you talk about what you're planning on doing with your draft? You could talk about why you circled part of it.

HENRY: I'm rereading my draft to see what I could do to make it better . . . I circled the ending because I want to work on it some more . . .

DANA: So what you're doing as a writer today is going back into your draft and rereading it to see what revisions you want to make. You've decided already that you need to work on your ending. [turns to class]

CHRIS: That was perfect. He told you exactly what he was doing.

ANIBAL: He told you what he was doing as a writer and not what he was going to write.

DANA: I'm going to give you time now to go off and write. While I confer with you today, I want you to think about what you could tell me right away that's going to let me know about the work that you are doing as a writer. Hold Sammy's and Henry's talk in your head as good examples to follow. One thing that might help is writing a self-assignment before you start writing. If you think your plans through carefully, you'll be more prepared.

There were several steps involved in Dana's coaching:

- As soon as she heard Henry talking about the content of his piece, she stopped the conference.
- She referred back to the conference with Sammy to remind Henry about how she wanted him to talk about his writing.
- Then she started the conference over, which gave Henry a chance to revise his response to her opening question.
- When Henry was unsure of what to say, Dana intervened and scaffolded his response by giving him some suggestions about what he might talk about.
- After Henry's second try, the class discussed what they had heard.
- Finally, Dana challenged the class to be prepared to talk the way she had helped Henry talk.

Dana followed these same steps to coach children to work on other aspects of their talk. For example, in a subsequent fishbowl, she felt that the student didn't use the class's writing discourse to describe his writing work. Just like she did with Henry, she stopped the conference and asked the student to repeat what he had said, this time using the vocabulary that the class used to describe their writing work. This fishbowl gave Dana an opportunity to teach her class that she wanted them to talk as precisely as possible about their writing work.

Supporting Student Talk During Conferences: The Crucial One-on-One Work

When a student talks about the content of his writing instead of his writing work, says little or nothing in response to our opening question, or describes his writing work in the most general terms, it's easy to conclude: *This kid can't talk about his writing.* At least it was for me during the first few years that I taught writing.

What I didn't yet understand during those years was that it was part of my job in a conference to teach students to fulfill their role in the conversation. Had I supported their talk, some students probably would have had more to say than I thought they did. And while it was true that some students didn't know how to talk about writing—not surprisingly, since most of them had never been in a writing workshop before—I could have taught them how as I conferred with them.

How, then, do we support—or even teach—talk as we confer with students? When I was first struggling to come up with an answer to this question, I recalled reading a book coauthored by Adele Faber and Elaine Mazlish, *How to Talk So Kids Will Listen and Listen So Kids Will Talk* (1980). While the book is written for parents and is not a book about the teaching of writing, I remembered that Faber and Mazlish recommend that parents use certain conversational strategies when they talk with their children, strategies that can help us nudge children to talk about their feelings or engage their cooperation. For example, the authors suggest that if we want to help children express their feelings, it helps to "Give the Feeling a Name" (15). ("My turtle is dead. He was alive this morning," says the child. "Oh no. What a shock," says the parent.) And the authors suggest that statements such as, "That's disgusting! Look at the apple cores on your bed. You live like a pig!" will probably not inspire children to cooperate with their parents. Instead, the authors suggest that using conversational strategies such as "Giving Information" ("Apple cores belong in the garbage") will help foster a spirit of cooperation (58).

Over the years, I've found there are conversational strategies we can use to help children talk about their writing work (see Figure 3–2). Many of these strategies are ones I use in my everyday conversations. All of us, in fact, use these strategies to initiate conversations and keep them going in our everyday give-and-take with friends and colleagues. Using them is as automatic to us as breathing.

For example, imagine you've just run into a friend on the street. You're excited to see her, because you've been wondering if she landed a job she had told you she had applied for. You start up the conversation by saying, "Good to see you. What's up?" She says quietly, "Oh, not too much." You say back what she just said, "Not too much, huh?" Then you pause for a moment, hoping that she'll say more. Without even thinking, you've just used a conversational strategy—reflecting back what someone says and then pausing with the expectation that the person you're talking to will fill in the silence with more talk—to get the conversation going.

But your friend sighs and say, "Same old, same old." You follow up by saying, "Last time we talked you said you were going to apply for that job at the college. What happened with that?" Again without

Conversational Strategy	Gives Support To	We Might Say . . .
Redirect	Students who talk about the content of their writing instead of their writing work.	"Your mom is really interesting. So what are you doing as a writer today?"
Reflect and Pause	Students who have some facility with talking about their writing work.	"So your writing is going okay . . ." "I see . . ."
Show and Describe		"Why don't you show me what you've been working on today, and describe what you're doing?"
Refer Back to the Last Conference		"Last time we talked you were working on your lead. Where are things now?"
Name What I've Observed		"I saw you were crossing out a section of your draft. Can you tell me what's going on?"
Take a Tour	Students who need a lot of support with talking about their writing work.	"I'm going to take a look at your draft, and describe what I think you're doing as a writer today."
Suggest Options		"So what are you doing as you draft—are you working on dialogue or internal thinking?"
Amplification	Students who need a demonstration of how to use writing discourse.	"Oh, I see. You're using *carets* to add words to your draft."
		"So you're using a *circular structure* to organize your memoir."
Ask for Clarification	Students who need practice using writing discourse.	"Could you explain what you mean by *stretching* your writing?"

FIGURE 3–2 Conversational strategies for helping students talk about their writing work

thinking, you've used a conversational strategy, this time by referring back to something you talked about in your last conversation to nudge your friend to say more. And this time, your friend tells you about what a disaster her job interview was.

Just as we do in our everyday conversations, we can use conversational strategies as we confer to help children talk about their writing work.

Redirecting Students Away From Talking About Content

At the beginning of the school year, when many students don't know we want them to talk about their writing work, it's common for some to respond to my opening by talking about the content of their writing. I usually respond by *redirecting* them toward talking about their writing work. That is, I change the subject. I listen to a student talk about content for a few moments, and often make a personal connection or respond to what the student is saying: "I had a rabbit when I was a boy, too," or "I'm sorry that you had to give your cat away." But then I gently shift the conversation toward what the child is doing as a writer.

CARL: How's it going?

JASON: Well, I'm writing about my dad. We go fishing.

CARL: Hmmm . . .

JASON: We caught three flounders this weekend. I got one myself!

CARL: Congratulations on catching that fish, Jason! So can you tell me about the work you're doing as a writer today?

JASON: [pauses for a moment] Well, I'm finished with my first draft. I want to get some talking in it, what my dad said when I caught the flounder.

Before I redirected Jason away from talking about the content of his fishing story, I was careful to respond enthusiastically to what he told me.

With some students, particularly those who are writing about difficult subjects, I redirect them as gently and respectfully as I can. For example, when I sat down to talk with Harry, a student in Barbara Rosenblum's second-grade classroom at P.S. 6 in Manhattan, he was working on a piece about the day his father had died of cancer the previous year (see Figure 3–3):

CARL: What are you doing as a writer, Harry?

HARRY: I'm writing about the day I found out my dad died . . .

CARL: So you're taking on a really . . .

HARRY: . . . sad . . .

The year before last my dad died!

After school for it is there that I found out that my dad died.

When I was about to go the Y, my mom was here so I went to her. She said, "Harry, I have some very, very SAD news." I said, "What Mom?" She said, "Papa died!" So we went to pick up Miller. My Mom told the news. Then we went to the Metropolitan's steps and cried with memories bunched in our heads.

FIGURE 3–3   First draft of Harry's piece about his dad

CARL: . . . and tough moment in your life. You're actually writing about the exact moment when you got the news?

HARRY: Yeah.

CARL: It takes a lot of courage to take something like that on in your writing, but one thing I know about you already this year, Harry, is that you approach your writing and your life with a lot of courage. You can really grapple with the tough things.

HARRY: [nods]

CARL: So what's your plan?

HARRY: I just started doing a better draft.

CARL: You're working on a *better* draft? What do you mean by that?

HARRY: Well, I've looked over it more, and I think I'll add some more dialogue.

I felt comfortable redirecting Harry because we had talked about his dad in another conference earlier that year when Harry was writing a poem about what his dad meant to him. I also knew that Harry wanted not just to write about his dad and his feelings about losing him, but he also wanted to write well about his dad.

Of course, I don't always redirect students away from talking about content. In some conferences, it's important I respond only as a human being at that moment, and then end the conversation.

For example, one cold winter day, when I asked Adriana, a seventh grader, how her writing was going, she burst into tears. Understandably so, because she was writing about her grandmother, who had passed away just a week earlier. How insensitive it would have been at that moment for me to say, "So, Adriana, your grandma died. I'm so sorry. Tell me about what you're doing as a writer today." Instead, I put an arm around her shoulder and said, "I'm so sorry that your grandma died, Adriana. That's really hard. Why don't you just keep writing, and we'll talk another time." There would be plenty of conferences in the future for me or Adriana's teacher to teach her about writing well. What she needed most on this day was to know I understood the seriousness of what she was writing about.

Supporting Students' Talk

I call them Calvin Coolidge conferences, after our former president who was famous for saying very little. I begin a conference with, "How's it going?" and the student responds, "Okay." Or I ask, "What work are you doing as a writer?" and the student says nothing.

A student who doesn't say much in response to our opening question may actually know how to talk about his writing work, and may even be quite good at this talk. He may not say too much, however, because we interrupted him when he was concentrating hard on his writing, and he needs a few moments to gather his thoughts before he can talk with us. He may lack confidence in his ability to talk well. Or he may feel nervous about talking with us, afraid to say the "wrong" thing.

Whatever the explanation, students sometimes need us to give them some support to help them talk about their writing work. I rely on four conversational strategies to give them this support.

Reflect and Pause   One way to nudge students to talk about their writing work is to use a conversational strategy I call *reflect and pause*. That is, I say back to the student what he's just said, and then I shut up and look expectantly at him for several seconds. Or I'll respond to the student with an "I see," or "Uh-huh," and then pause, often as a way of keeping the conversation going once the student has started talking about what he's doing.

I used both variations of this strategy to support the talk of Abby, a sixth grader:

CARL: Hi, Abby. How's it going?

ABBY: Fine.

CARL: *So it's going fine . . .*

ABBY: Well . . . I've been working on the draft . . .

CARL: *Uh-huh . . .*

ABBY: Except I keep finding that what I'm writing doesn't make enough sense . . . so I keep going back and making changes again and again. I never realized how complicated it was to write a memoir. I'm trying to make my beginning like "Eleven" [by Sandra Cisneros]. But I'm not used to saying what my memories mean to me, so it's hard for me to figure out what to say in my beginning.

CARL: Let me see if I can say this back in a way that makes sense. You like how Sandra Cisneros starts "Eleven" by telling us what the story means, but you're having trouble figuring out what your memories mean so you can do the same thing in your beginning.

ABBY: Yeah.

The most important component of this strategy is the pause that follows, a pause that gives students a chance to collect their thoughts. I've learned not to be nervous about these silences, and instead see them as opportunities to sing a Beatles song in my head. My silence also communicates to students that I expect them to talk, so if I jump back too soon into the conversation, I let them off the hook.

Show and Describe   I've found that some students are able to talk about their writing work after they hold their writing in their hands and look it over for a few moments, a strategy I call *show and describe*. The act of picking up their work and flipping through its pages gives them some time to think, and reminds them of the work they've been doing. Here I used the strategy with Eddie, a fourth grader:

CARL: How's it going?

EDDIE: Good.

CARL: So it's going good . . .

EDDIE: [nods]

CARL: *Eddie, why don't you show me your draft, and tell me what you're doing as a writer.*

EDDIE: [picks up his draft] Well, I'm working on my draft . . .

CARL: I see . . .

EDDIE: [looks intently at the page he was working on] I want to put thinking in this part . . . when Michael gets sent to his room.

CARL: So you want to include the thoughts of your main character
    when he gets punished?
EDDIE: [nods]

Refer Back to the Last Conference   Some students simply don't
know where to start when we ask about the work they're doing as writers. We can support these children's talk by *referring back to the last conference* we had with them. When we use this strategy, we give students
a place to start talking about their writing work.

I used this strategy with Ishador, a second grader, and hit pay dirt.

CARL: So how's it going, Ishador?
ISHADOR: [doesn't say anything]
CARL: *Ishador, I remember last time we talked, you were going to make a
    book like* One of Three *[by Angela Johnson], and write about sev-
    eral memories you have of your grandma. What are you doing now?*
ISHADOR: [thinks for a moment] Writing about her cooking for me.
CARL: You're writing about her cooking for you . . .
ISHADOR: I'm seeing it in my head.
CARL: You're trying to get a picture in your head of your grandmother
    cooking before you write about her?
ISHADOR: Yeah.

In order to refer back to the last conference I had with a child, I
need to know what we talked about a week ago, or even longer. I'm
able to use the strategy because I'm in the habit of skimming over my
notes before each conference.

Naming What I've Observed   As I walk over to a student, I try to notice things he's doing as he writes. He might, for example, be rereading
entries in his writers notebook. He might be studying a model piece of
literature the class has read. Or he might be crossing out a section of his
draft.

I can nudge a student to talk about his writing work by *naming
what I've observed*. Here I used the strategy with Alex, a first grader.

CARL: How's it going, Alex?
ALEX: Fine.
CARL: *Alex, I see that you've taped a strip of blank paper to the bottom of
    your story. Could you tell me why?*
ALEX: [thinks a moment] I want to add on to my story. I want to tell
    about what my puppy looks like.

CARL: Oh, so you're adding on to your story, and you taped the paper
on the bottom to give you more room.
ALEX: Yeah.

Teaching Students to Talk About Their Writing Work
In some conferences, we give students support to help them talk, and
they still don't say anything about their writing work. This may be because they have little experience talking about their writing. Or it may
be that students are trying new strategies or techniques in their writing
they've learned in our mini-lessons, or from their classmates in peer
conferences, and they aren't quite sure how to explain what they're
doing.

There are two conversational strategies we can use to teach these
students how to talk about their writing work.

Taking a Tour   We've all had conversations with friends or relatives in
which we say to them, "You've got the biggest smile I've ever seen on
your face. Tell me, what's the good news?" or "Have you been crying?
What's the matter?" From looking closely at them and "reading" their
expressions or body language, we make guesses about what's going on
with them, and then we ask them to confirm our guesses.

Likewise, when I'm conferring with a student who isn't able to
talk about his writing work, I'll *take a tour* of his writing—that is, I'll
quickly skim his writers notebook or draft and look for evidence of the
work he's doing as a writer. Has the student written just a few lines of
his draft, indicating that he's writing a lead? Are there arrows leading
from text to the margins, telling me that the student may be adding information? Has the student circled misspelled words, indicating that he
may be editing for spelling? Once I think I know what work the student
is doing, I'll ask him to confirm my hunch.

I used the take-a-tour strategy with Shenita, an eighth grader in
Wes Flinn's class in M.S. 51 in Brooklyn:

CARL: How's it going?
SHENITA: Fine.
CARL: So it's going fine?
SHENITA: Yeah.
CARL: *Shenita, I'm going to take a tour of your writing and see what kind
of work you've been doing. [I skim over her draft. See Figure 3–4.] I
see that you've circled several sections of your draft.*
SHENITA: [nods]

After I graduated from 6th grade, my class and I had to return to school to get our report cards. My friend brought ~~to~~ a sad tape to school about friends leaving each other. She put the tape in the tape recorder and my friends and I started to ~~were~~ ~~crying~~. We were crying because we were leaving each other. As I was crying I ~~was~~ remembered the times when ~~my~~ friends and I were at lunch talking about the various things that happen through the week. As the tape was playing me and my friends were hugging each other and we were telling each other how we would miss one ~~other~~ another. We were talking about graduation. On graduation we were taking pictures of each other, we were also talking about how sad it was that this kids father died on the day of graduation. On the last day of school we were signing each other's year books. Also, on the last day of school we were talking about the fun trips we were on. After I graduated and left that school I went to summer camp and some of my friends from the school were there also. After that summer camp I haven't seen them again but I talk to them on the phone sometimes.

FIGURE 3–4   First draft of Shenita's piece about her sixth-grade graduation

CARL: *I see each of these sections is a flashback to one of your sixth-grade memories. So are you going to revise these sections?*
SHENITA: Yeah.
CARL: Could you say back to me what you're doing?
SHENITA: [pauses for a moment] Well, I'm revising . . .
CARL: Uh-huh.
SHENITA: I'm going to stretch these parts out.

Once Shenita confirmed my hunch, I was able to proceed with the conference (which focused on how to write well-developed flashbacks). The strategy also helped me teach Shenita how she could talk about what she was doing. Not only did telling Shenita what I thought she was doing as a writer give her a chance to confirm my hunch, it gave her a quick demonstration of writers' talk. And then I gave her an opportunity to practice that talk by saying back to me what she was doing.

The taking-a-tour strategy is a particularly useful one when we confer with primary students who haven't yet learned to talk well about their writing. Especially in the beginning of the school year, kindergarteners and first graders often begin conferences by telling me about the content of their pieces, and when I redirect them to tell me about their writing work, they look at me with puzzled expressions. In these conferences, I respond by saying, "You know what I'm going to do now? I'm going to look at your writing. I have a feeling you're doing so many things that writers do, and I'm going to look for those things, and tell you what I find out." Then, as I look at their work, I give a running commentary of what I see: "Oh, I see you're making a picture book . . . I see you're really trying to spell some hard words and put spaces between your words . . . Oh, and look here, you added a Post-it to this page so you could add some more writing to your book!" This kind of commentary is the kind of demonstration of writers' talk that helps our youngest students learn how to talk like writers.

I should note that I also use the taking-a-tour strategy with students who I know *can* talk about their writing work, but who resist talking with me. When I taught seventh and eighth graders, for example, I discovered that many adolescents simply don't want to talk with teachers, especially when their peers are watching. At times, some of my thirteen- and fourteen-year-old students were openly hostile to the idea of having conversations with me about their writing, and calculated that if they didn't say anything, I would go away. While I was sometimes tempted to walk away, I used the taking-a-tour strategy to figure out what they were doing as writers, and to give me the information I needed to proceed with the conference.

Suggesting Possibilities   When I take a tour of a student's writing, it isn't always so clear to me what a student is trying to do in his writing. Not every piece of writing will conveniently contain arrows or circling or cross-outs that are indicators of certain kinds of writing work.

When there isn't any obvious evidence of a student's writing work, I *suggest possibilities*. When I use this strategy, I think back to the kinds of writing work that I've been talking about in recent mini-lessons. Then I list them and ask the student if he's doing any of these things.

Using this strategy helped me figure out the work that Maryann, a third grader, was doing as she worked on a poem.

CARL: How's it going?
MARYANN: Fine.
CARL: So it's going fine . . . Maryann, I see you're working on a poem about your kitten.
MARYANN: [nods]
CARL: *We've been talking the past several days about how poets break their lines. We've talked about how poets use white space. And we've talked about how and why poets repeat lines. Are you doing some of this work in this poem?*
MARYANN: Yes.
CARL: What have you been doing?
MARYANN: Line breaks . . . I've been working on line breaks.

Conversational Strategies That Support Students' Use of Writing Discourse

I find that students who talk about their writing work don't always talk with precision. Consequently, it's sometimes not entirely clear to me what it is they're doing. For example, a student who tells me "I'm fixing my draft" could be talking about revision or editing. And when it's not clear to me what a child is doing, it's hard for me to get on a line of thinking about a student's writing work.

When we are conferring with a student, and his talk is imprecise, we have a perfect opportunity to teach him the discourse he needs to communicate clearly with us, and with other writers. Two conversational strategies can help us do this important teaching.

Ask for Clarification   When a student's description of his writing work confuses me, I *ask for clarification*. I'll use a phrase like "What do you mean by . . ." and then repeat the part of the student's description that confused me.

In a conference with Jasmine, a fourth grader, I nudged her to talk more precisely about her writing work.

CARL: How's it going?

JASMINE: I finished my first draft. Now I'm going to make some changes, and stuff.

CARL: What do you mean by "make some changes"?

JASMINE: I'm going to do some revisions.

CARL: And by *revisions* you mean . . .

JASMINE: You know, adding stuff into my draft.

CARL: Oh, so you're doing some adding-on work.

JASMINE: Yeah.

When I ask for clarification, I nudge a student to reach for writing discourse she may have heard me or classmates use, but that she herself hasn't yet made part of her usual way of talking about her writing. Jasmine went from saying she was going to "make some changes" to "do some revisions" to "adding stuff into my draft." Each time I asked for clarification, the words she used became more and more precise. As a result, I got the information I needed to know—that I should focus the rest of the conference on how she was adding on to her draft. And I hoped that after getting some practice with using words of writing discourse like "revisions" and "adding," Jasmine would continue to use them in future conversations about her writing.

Amplification When a student talks imprecisely about his writing work but I'm pretty sure I know what he's doing in his writing, I use a strategy I call *amplification*. That is, I'll say back what the student told me, but use writing discourse to name what he's doing.

In a conference with Daniel, a fifth grader, I amplified his talk:

CARL: How's it going?

DANIEL: I'm finished with it. I think I'm going to make some changes.

CARL: You mean you're finished with your *first draft*?

DANIEL: Yup.

CARL: And you're going to work on *revisions*?

DANIEL: Yup. I'm gonna make a better beginning.

CARL: Oh, so you're going to work on your *lead*.

DANIEL: Yup.

When I amplify what a child like Daniel says, I'm demonstrating how to use words of writing discourse like *first draft* and *revision* and *lead* in the appropriate context. I hope that he'll make these words his own in future conferences.

TWELVE YEARS AFTER launching my first writing workshop, I still can't wait to confer with students when I arrive at the schools where I work. I still can't wait to have the kinds of in-depth conversations I read about in *The Art of Teaching Writing* years ago, the kinds in which students talk fluently and with precision about their writing work.

I still have conferences with students who respond by saying "okay" or with silence after I ask, "How's it going?" I no longer give up in these conferences, or on these students. I know that I can draw from a repertoire of strategies to support students' talk, or even to teach them how to talk like writers. And I know that I can suggest to these students' teachers that they immerse their students in the conference conversation wherever possible, and teach mini-lessons about how to talk in conferences. And weeks or months later, when I confer with these students again, I am usually pleased to find out that these students are learning to talk like writers.

References

Calkins, Lucy. 1986. *The Art of Teaching Writing* (First Edition). Portsmouth, NH: Heinemann.

Cambourne, Brian. 1988. *The Whole Story.* New York: Scholastic.

Cisneros, Sandra. 1991. *Woman Hollering Creek.* New York: Vintage Books.

Faber, Adele, and Elaine Mazlish. 1980. *How to Talk So Kids Will Listen and Listen So Kids Will Talk.* New York: Avon.

Greenfield, Eloise, and Lessie Jones Little. 1979. *Childtimes: A Three-Generation Memoir.* New York: Crowell.

Johnson, Angela. 1991. *One of Three.* New York: Orchard.

Smith, Frank. 1995. *Between Hope and Havoc.* Portsmouth, NH: Heinemann.

Matchmaker, Matchmaker

4

Teaching Students to Learn from Authors

I'm going to share a secret with you. Ralph Fletcher, the author of *What a Writer Needs, Fig Pudding,* and many other wonderful books, is my personal writing mentor. Ralph is available to help me with my writing at any hour of the day, every day of the week. And he's cheap. Let me explain how this arrangement came about—and how you, too, can have Ralph Fletcher as your personal writing mentor.

I had a lot of trouble getting started with the first chapter of this book. Although I had gathered a lot of ideas in my writers notebook, I had no clue about how to organize them into a draft. After several false starts and stretches of time when I stared at my laptop screen so long the computer put itself in "sleep" mode, I decided to look at how other educators had written the first chapter of their books on the teaching of writing. When I picked up Ralph Fletcher's *What a Writer Needs* (1993), I was struck by how Ralph introduces the subject of his first chapter—mentors—by telling several personal stories. In the sections that follow, Ralph discusses the qualities of a good mentor.

As I read Ralph's chapter, I got an idea of how I could set up my own chapter. To introduce the chapter's subject—the characteristics of the conference conversation—I could start by telling a personal story. Then, in several sections that would follow, I could discuss those characteristics one by one. I put Ralph's book down, sketched out an outline for the chapter in my writers notebook, and started drafting.

That evening, Ralph taught me a valuable lesson about a way to structure an introductory chapter. As I wrote other chapters, I returned to *What a Writer Needs* to learn other craft lessons. The cost of all these lessons? The price of the book, which equalled the cost of an inexpensive dinner for two in New York City. For being such an available and affordable writing mentor, I say to you, Ralph Fletcher, thanks.

We hope our students will become the kind of writers who also have such writing mentors. They read their favorite authors' books and essays and poems with a "writer's eye" and notice how these authors craft their writing. When students read poems like Eloise Greenfield's

"Honey, I Love," they notice that poets create rhythm by repeating lines. When they read picture books like Nick Butterworth's *My Dad Is Awesome,* they learn that one way a writer can reveal his theme is by stating it clearly in the first line of his book ("My dad is awesome."), and circling back to it in the last line ("He's awesome!"). Then, in their own writing, students try out the craft techniques they've noticed.

The main focus of this chapter is on the crucial one-on-one work we do in conferences to teach students to have and learn from writing mentors. There are some predictable steps we can take when we are conferring with students who have mentors, and with those who don't.

Our teaching in these conferences has two goals. First, we help students learn something about crafting their writing—how to write a character's thoughts, how to make time transitions, how to structure a piece. Second, and perhaps more important than the specific craft techniques we help students learn, we show students how to learn from writing mentors. In *Wondrous Words,* Katie Wood Ray (1999) describes these conferences as opportunities to teach students how to inquire into craft:

> You might have noticed that the essential components of the line of thinking for inquiry [into craft] are all "covered" in subtle ways in a conference like this . . . . When we follow this predictable line in our teaching, we are doing more than helping students with a certain piece of writing at a certain time. Our ways of working with them also serve as consistent demonstrations of how to learn to write from writers. (252)

When we are successful in showing students how to learn from writing mentors, we teach students how to teach themselves. While our writing workshops inevitably end in June, students can continue to go to texts written by their favorite authors and learn craft lessons to help them write better.

To have conferences in which we teach students how to learn from writing mentors, we need to have a collection of texts to talk about with students. This chapter also includes a discussion of how to assemble such a collection.

Initiating a Conversation About Writing Mentors
During the first part of conferences, I often learn that students are doing craft work (see Figure 4–1). Immediately, a question pops into my mind: "Does this student have a writing mentor from whom she's learned to do this work?" I know that if students have mentors—and I

TYPES OF CRAFT WORK	EXAMPLES OF TECHNIQUES
Structuring a Piece	Circle Series of Vignettes
Writing Leads	Dialogue Action
Writing Endings	Ambiguous Summation
Making Transitions	Subheadings White Space
Constructing a Scene	Dialogue Inner Thinking
Description	Telling Details Simile
Emphasis	Short Sentences Repetition
Create Sound	Onomatopoeia Alliteration

FIGURE 4–1   Some kinds of craft work

am familiar with them—then I'll have a clear image of what they are try-ing to reach for in their writing. If I am not familiar with students' men-tors, I'll be able to get an image of what they're trying to do by taking a few moments to skim the texts, or by asking students to explain what they've learned from studying them.

When we refer again and again in mini-lessons to texts we love, it's not unusual for students to tell me—without any prompting—that the authors of those texts are their mentors. Optimally, when students describe their craft work, they tell me which favorite text they are using as a model, what they've learned from studying it, and how and where they're using what they've learned in their own writing.

Of course, when students tell me about their craft work, not all of them will say they have a writing mentor. As I pursue my line of think-ing about the work these students are doing, I'll ask them a few of these research questions:

- Who is your writing mentor?
- Is there a text you are using as a model?
- Where did you learn how to do this craft work?
- What did you learn from your writing mentor?
- How are you using your model text to help you write better?

Even when I'm certain a student doesn't have a writing mentor, I may still ask if he does. After all, the research questions we ask students are informed by what we know good writers do. Since I know that good writers use other authors' writing as models for their own, I ask this question as a way of letting students know I expect they will be-come the kind of writers who have writing mentors.

As early as I can in a conference, then, I establish whether or not students have writing mentors. If a student does have a mentor, then there are some predictable steps I take in the rest of the conference. If a student doesn't, there are a few additional steps.

Teaching Students Who Already Have Writing Mentors

When I first started conferring, only an occasional student would refer to a text as the source for an idea of how she might write her ending or create sounds in her writing. These students left me speechless. Since I had not been taught how to apprentice myself to writing mentors when I was a child (or a young adult, for that matter), I felt inadequate in these conferences. I told these students I was incredibly impressed they had writing mentors and left them to continue writing—without teaching them anything. I wondered what else I could teach them that

Donald Crews or Jean Little or Gary Soto hadn't already taught them to do.

Today, I'm still impressed by students who tell me they have writing mentors, but I'm not at a loss for words anymore when I confer with them. I've learned that my primary job in these conferences is to teach these students how to learn from their writing mentors.

In some conferences, for example, students haven't yet done the craft work inspired by a writing mentor. In these conferences, I help students envision how they can apply what they noticed in a mentor text to the writing they are about to do.

One morning, I conferred with Natalie, a student in Nicole Harris's second-grade classroom in P.S. 6 in Manhattan. During the past few days, Natalie had written several entries in her writers notebook about her dad, and she was now deciding how to organize her material into a picture book.

CARL: Hi, Natalie. How's it going today?

NATALIE: I'm making a picture book.

CARL: Okay . . .

NATALIE: Well, I'm trying to decide where I should, like, make the pages . . .

CARL: What do you mean, "make the pages"?

NATALIE: Well, I'm gonna try to make this entry page number one because it's not really a memory, it's really a description. [See Figure 4–2A.] So I'm going to make that on the first page and then . . . [She flips through the pages of her notebook for a few moments.]

CARL: So you're thinking about what's going to go on each page of your picture book. Is there a picture book you want yours to be like?

NATALIE: *When I Was Young in the Mountains* [by Cynthia Rylant]. After my last publishing [a few weeks earlier], I read the book again and I figured out that if we publish again, I'm probably going to use this book.

CARL: Can I take a look at your entries?

NATALIE: Uh-huh.

CARL: [I skim the entries Natalie has written about her dad.] You know, the kind of stuff you have in your notebook—lots of stories about your dad—reminds me of the kind of stuff that Cynthia Rylant has in her book.

How helpful it was for me to learn that Natalie wanted to make a picture book like *When I Was Young in the Mountains,* which contains several poignant memories of an Appalachian childhood. Since I knew the book well, I knew right away what Natalie wanted to make—a book that would contain a series of memories about her dad. When I looked at the entries in Natalie's writers notebook, I saw she had the material she needed to make a similar book.

To teach Natalie, I had her take a close look at *When I Was Young in the Mountains* to get a clear image in her mind of how the text is organized. I wanted Natalie to have a solid understanding of the organizational structure that Rylant had used to make her book, *and* I also wanted her to learn that writers often study their mentor texts before they write. Natalie, after all, hadn't looked at *When I Was Young in the Mountains* for several weeks.

CARL: I'd like to help you figure out how your book is going to go. So let's take a look at *When I Was Young in the Mountains* and see how Cynthia Rylant puts the book together. I'd like you to tell me what you've noticed about the way Cynthia Rylant made this book. That can help you figure out how yours might go. Where is the book? [Natalie goes and gets the book from the basket of mentor texts in the classroom library.]

NATALIE: [skims the first few pages of the book] She has, like, different stories that go with the pictures and it just keeps going with different stories . . . On the first page of the story her grandpop comes home and kisses her on the forehead . . . Then there's the one about okra.

CARL: So she keeps going with different stories. That's a good thing to have noticed, that she tells several stories in the book. How are you going to do what Cynthia Rylant did—"keep going with different stories"?

NATALIE: The entry I'm not going to use is the sock fight [Figure 4–2C]. No one will know what it is. It will probably sound a little weird anyway.

CARL; Okay, so what entries are you going to use?

NATALIE: Well, I was suggesting this entry [Figure 4–2A] be page one.

CARL: That's the entry about how you love your daddy, how you feel about him, right?

NATALIE: Yeah.

CARL: You know, Cynthia Rylant has a page like that in *When I Was Young in the Mountains*. See here? [I turn to the last page.] She ends the book by telling us how she feels about the mountains. You want to tell your feelings about your dad, but you want to put it in the front.

NATALIE: [nods]

CARL: What might be a good second page?

NATALIE: Maybe this one on climbing the rocks . . . I'll make that page two. [See Figure 4–2D.]

CARL: And the next page?

NATALIE: This one, on playing soccer. [See Figure 4–2F.]

CARL: Natalie, what I think is so smart about your thinking today is that you reread all the stuff you've written about your dad and you decided on the kind of thing you want to make, you want to make a picture book. Not only that, there's a certain picture book you thought of to help you think about how yours can go. Just like Cynthia Rylant puts a lot of stories together in a row, you're going to do the same thing in your book. You've learned a lot from Cynthia Rylant.

NATALIE: [nods]

CARL: I'd like you to keep rereading your entries and decide how the rest of your picture book is going to go. Then get started with your draft.

NATALIE: Okay.

When I checked in with Natalie later on in the period, she had finished planning out the sequence of pages in her picture book and had started drafting. And, instead of returning *When I Was Young in the Mountains* to the classroom library, she had kept it right next to her on her table so she could look at it again as she worked.

When students tell me they have a writing mentor, but they haven't yet done the work inspired by the mentor, I take these steps to help them imagine how to apply what they've learned from their mentor to their own writing:

- If they don't have a copy of their mentor text beside them, I ask them to get it out of their desk, or find a copy in the classroom.
- If I am unfamiliar with the text, I skim it.
- I ask students to describe the craft work done by their mentor author.
- If students have trouble describing the craft work, I'll point out what the mentor author has done.
- During the "have-a-go," I nudge students to talk out how they're going to use what they've learned from their mentor in their own writing.

In other conferences, students have already used what they learned from a mentor text in their writing. I've learned that it's one thing for

A   1

I love my daddy because
he loves me. He loves me because
I am cute and smart. Me and my
dad spend a lot of time togeth
er, like drawing... wrestling... playing
and Just having fun. Me and my
dad have alot in common too!
We both like cats, we both
like animals.

If my daddy weren't alive
I would be sad. I think my dad
is the best dad to walk the
earth. One of the reasons
are because he comes home
early just because I want
to goto the park and play
base ball. If my dad weren't
alive I wouldn't be happy.

B   2

When I went to florida the
first thing I did was go in the
pool. The pool is my favorite place
because it is very hot in florida
but the pool cools me off.
When I was in the pool my
brother came in and started
chasing me all over. Then
my dad came in and major
splashed my brother. My mom
and grandma say my dad is
a pool splasher. So me spencer
and dad played tag and wrestling
I was on my dad's side when
we wrestled!

C   3

When me and my dad have
a sock fight we hit each
other. My dad cheats
by crossing the bed. Sock
fight is when you throw
socks at each other but
only my dads socks.
Sometimes my brother
joins in. In sock fight
I always win.

Me and my dad just wish
we could have a cat. Me and
my dad want a silky soft
smooth velvety black and
white cat. My dad wants
a black and white cat
because he used to
have one but it died.

D   4

Sometimes my dad comes
home early and we go to
the park to climb rocks.
My dad isn't as great
at rock climbing then
I am but I still love him.
When we go rock climbing
we eat either Ice cream
or Icea. When we climb
rocks I always go first
to lead my dad. Me and
my dad hopped around the
rocks and slide down them.
Me and my dad just love it
Sometimes my dad gets
worried when I don't
need him but I don't
care one bit. I am happy
he cares So after we
hopped around rocks and
got to the easy stuff we

FIGURE 4–2 Natalie's notebook entries about her dad [A through D]

came to a ledge. Somtimes
I need help so my dad
is always there to help me
then I help my dad up.
After we just hang out untill
we need to go home. When
we get home I thank
my dad for a great
time. This is one of the
reasons I love my dad
because he spends
time with me.

When me and my dad
play with my crabs we have
fun. I used to have one
named Jeffery. When we
play with my crabs I feel
responsible for taking care
of my pets. Jeffery was

always my favorite
crab. That night me
and my dad played
school It think that
was the night we
found out that he was
dead

Sometimes me and
my dad play soccer
in the hall. My dad says
to wear shoes because
when we kick the
ball it hurts our feet.
I always block my dad
but sometimes he scores
just a little though. I
score a lot. Sometimes I
think about my best
year. my first year we won
every game except the

last thats how I got
so good. My gole was
to the middle and my dads
goal was at the 2 doors
in the hallway. We had
our goals and then the
game begins. Yes I got
three points.

FIGURE 4–2   (Continued) Natalie's notebook entries about her dad [E through G] students to notice the way a favorite author writes a lead or uses just the right words to evoke a setting, and quite another for them to use these techniques skillfully. When writers learn a new technique, after all, they rarely pull it off well on the first try. Rather, they make an approximation of the technique, often falling way short of what their writing mentors have done. There's almost always something else to teach students to help them make better approximations of the technique.

In these conferences, instead of giving the students critical feedback, I "ask" the mentor to give it. That is, I have students compare what they've written to their mentor's writing. In many conferences, students will notice something about the way their mentor used a craft technique that they haven't done as well in their writing.

In fifth-grade teacher Bonnie Stalzer's class at Lakeside School in Merrick, Long Island, Bonnie and her students had studied several well-crafted texts. Many of the students were using craft techniques in their writing that they had learned during the study. When I conferred with Jennifer, who was writing a memoir about her grandmother's birthday party, I found out she was using a technique for showing the passage of time that she had learned from Cynthia Rylant's *The Relatives Came*. In the book, Rylant shows time passing by referring several times to grapes growing on a vine, grapes that are riper each time they are mentioned.

CARL: So how's it going, Jennifer?

JENNIFER: Good. On my draft I'm repeating the sun. In the beginning, I wrote, "One June afternoon, when the sun was really bright." At the end, I wrote, "It was almost dark, and the sun could hardly be seen."

CARL: So you write about the sun in a couple of places in your draft, and you change the image at the end of the story . . .

JENNIFER: Yeah, like the grapes in *The Relatives Came*. I'm using the sun because it gives you a picture of what time of day it is.

CARL: I see.

JENNIFER. I'm trying to show how time changed in my story. See, in the beginning you could still see the sun—it was daytime—and at the end it was starting to become night, and you couldn't see the sun anymore.

CARL: So you've mentioned the sun twice in your piece, at the beginning and at the end, and changed the image to show time passing.

JENNIFER: Yeah.

CARL: So let me take a close look at your beginning and ending. [I read both parts. See Figure 4–3.]

> One June afternoon when
> the sun was still very bright,
> the Rosners made their way
> down a long road to where
> a party for their grandmother
> would be held.
>
>
> It was almost dark and the
> sun could hardly be seen.
> We drove all the way home
> thinking of next year and
> the fun we would have!

FIGURE 4–3   Lead and ending of Jennifer's piece about her grandmother's birthday

It was valuable for me to know that Cynthia Rylant was Jennifer's writing mentor. Since I knew *The Relatives Came* inside and out, I knew what Jennifer was trying to pull off. And I also knew what I could teach Jennifer to deepen her understanding of the technique she was using for showing the passage of time—where Rylant mentions the grapes ripening several times across the piece, Jennifer used it only twice, at the beginning and the end of her story.

Instead of telling this to Jennifer, however, I nudged her to look again at her copy of *The Relatives Came*, and compare how she used the technique to what Rylant does. That is, I let Rylant "give" Jennifer critical feedback.

CARL: Where's your copy of *The Relatives Came*?

JENNIFER: [looks for her copy of the text and finds it in her writing folder]

CARL: Take a look at the places where Cynthia Rylant mentions the grapes. I see you underlined those places already. See if you see anything that she did with the grapes that you might still try with the sun.

JENNIFER: [studies the text for a few moments] Well, she mentions the grapes four times. She did it twice near the beginning, once in the middle, and once at the end.

CARL: So she talks about the grapes throughout the book. Holding up the book next to your draft, do you get any ideas for what you could do in your writing?

JENNIFER: Yeah . . . I don't just have to do the sun in the beginning and the end. I can do it in the middle.

CARL: And why would you do that?

JENNIFER: To show time passing some more.

CARL: That sounds like a good idea. That might help people reading your story to get a better sense of how time is moving along during all of your draft, not just when they get to the end. So where do you think you might want to weave another image of the sun into your piece?

JENNIFER: [skims her draft for a few moments and finally points to a part several pages into her draft] Here.

CARL: You've got a good plan, Jennifer. I like how looking back at your mentor piece helped you get some more ideas for how you can use this technique of showing time passing. I'll check back with you later this period to see how you're doing with this.

When she returned to her draft after the conference, Jennifer carried out her plan (see Figure 4–4). Not only did Jennifer learn more about using this particular technique, but—more important—she learned she could return to a model text and learn from it again and again.

Of course, not all students will be able to see a way to deepen their work with a craft technique by looking back at their model text. Sometimes that's because they need more time to study the text than the few short moments a conference allows. In some conferences, then, I ask a student to spend some time—five or ten minutes—carefully rereading the parts of the text where the author uses the craft technique. Later in the period, when he's through rereading, I continue the conference.

Now if you had looked out the window you would have seen that the sun was still shining over everything and had turned an orange color that always makes you feel warm inside on a long Spring evening.

FIGURE 4–4   Jennifer's revision work

Sometimes a student doesn't notice anything else about using a craft technique from looking back at a model text. When this is the case, I give the student critical feedback and teach him about how he can do his craft work better by pointing out what I've noticed about the way the author uses the technique. Then I'll nudge the student to try it that way in his writing. Let's say that Jennifer hadn't noticed how Cynthia Rylant mentions the grapes in several places in the story. I might then have said to her:

> Here's what I'm seeing, Jennifer. You let us know at the beginning of your story that it's mid-afternoon, because the sun "is still very bright." And at the end of your story you let us know that it's late evening, because "it was almost dark and the sun could hardly be seen." I noticed in *The Relatives Came* that Cynthia Rylant gives us information about time passing not just in the beginning and end of her story, but in the middle, too. I'd like you to try this, too. Try giving your readers more information about time passing, just like Rylant does.

121

I have had conferences in which I'm not sure what I should teach students to deepen their understanding of how to use a craft technique. When this happens, students' writing mentors usually save the day for me. As students revisit their mentor texts, I look at the texts alongside them. Often, as I read, I'll see something else students can do to use a craft technique better. In these conferences, the writing mentor teaches both the student *and* me. And there have been conferences where students have noticed a way they can use a craft technique that I hadn't seen. Many students have enjoyed teaching me something they learned from taking another look at a mentor text.

When students have already done the craft work inspired by a writing mentor, I take the following steps to help them learn more from their writing mentor:

- I ask students to take another look at how their writing mentor used the craft technique, and compare what they notice to how they used the technique in their own writing.
- If students notice something that their mentor did that they haven't done, then I ask them to try it in their own writing.
- If students don't see anything else in the text, then I point out what their mentor did that they haven't, and then ask them to try it in their own writing.

Teaching Students Who Don't Yet Have Writing Mentors

Not every student will have a mentor text in mind when they're crafting their writing. A student may not realize there is, in fact, a text the class has already looked at that might give her ideas for how she might craft her writing. A student may feel the texts the class has read and studied don't address the craft issues she's grappling with, and may be unsure of where to find another text that does. Or the student may not realize the benefits of having a writing mentor. My job in these conferences is to match the student up to an appropriate text, and teach her how to craft her writing better by using the text as an example.

Wherever possible, I try to match students up to texts their class has already read and studied in mini-lessons. Let's say a student is trying to write dialogue. If she doesn't have a specific model text in mind, then it's my job to remember a text the class has read that contains dialogue. That way, I can say to her, "Remember how in that Jean Little piece we read she gets her characters talking? Let's look back at the story. I'll bet you might get some ideas you can use to make your lead work better."

Once I've matched up students to a familiar text, the second part of the conference proceeds much the same as in those conferences where students already have writing mentors. I ask students to compare their writing to the text, and then try out what they learn from the text in their writing.

In some conferences, however, I am unable to think of a text the class has read that would help students learn about the craft technique they are using. In this case, I have no choice but to match students up to a text they are not familiar with. This kind of conference presents some special challenges.

For example, one afternoon in Andrea Clark's classroom at Derby Ridge Elementary School in Columbia, Missouri, her fifth graders were writing poetry. When I conferred with Kamara about the poem she was writing about a basketball game, I found out that she was trying to create a sense of movement in one part of the poem.

CARL: So what are you doing as a poet today, Kamara?
KAMARA: Well, on this part where it says "So, I'lll *PASS IT . . . ,*" I make the words slant this way because I was passing. The words, they're supposed to be kinda leaning over. [See Figure 4–5.]
CARL: [I lean over and skim the poem so I can see what Kamara's talking about.] Leaning over . . . You're trying to make the words lean over . . . Do you want people to feel like there's movement in your poem, like the ball is moving through the air?
KAMARA: [nods]
CARL: Kamara, is there a poet you've been reading who has been helping you think about ways to create movement in your poem?
KAMARA: No.
CARL: I'm curious . . . How did you know to lean these words over?
KAMARA: [shrugs] Well, I kinda made it up.
CARL: Wow, so today you invented your own way of creating movement in your poem.
KAMARA: [smiles] I guess.

Because Kamara didn't have any poems in mind in which the authors had tried to create movement, I couldn't take her back to those poems to help her learn more about this kind of craft work. As I thought about the poems Ms. Clark had read the class, I couldn't think of any in which the authors had tried to create movement. But in the anthology I had with me, *Pterodactyls and Pizza*, edited by Lee Bennet Hopkins, I remembered that the poet Bobbi Katz creates a feeling of movement in her poem "Spring Is" (see Figure 4–6). Instead of putting

BASKETBALL!

My first time playing

THE GAME

In front of an audience

CONFUSED...

Are we playing offense or defense? Why am I the only one at this end of the court.?

OK I got the ball soo I'll PASS IT. The ball is going going going to the other team Is that what they mean by

BAD PASSES!

FIGURE 4–5   First draft of Kamara's "Basketball!"

Spring Is

Spring is when
    the morning sputters like
bacon
    and
      your
        sneakers
        run
         down
          the
           stairs
so fast you can hardly keep up with them,
and
spring is when
    your scrambled eggs
      jump
        off
        the
         plate
and turn into a million daffodils
trembling in the sunshine.

Bobbi Katz

FIGURE 4–6   "Spring Is" by Bobbi Katz

the words she uses to describe running down the stairs or scrambled eggs jumping off a plate on single lines, Katz writes one word per line, and indents each word further and further across the page.

However, I knew Kamara was probably unfamiliar with the poem. Introducing Kamara to "Spring Is" would pose some extra challenges in this conference.

CARL: I like how you've created movement by slanting words, Kamara. I'm going to show you another way of doing this, because the more ways we know how to do something in a poem, the more of a chance we can get the poem to do exactly what we want it to do. [I reach into my carry bag for my copy of *Pterodactyls and Pizza*.] I'm going to show you Bobbi Katz's poem "Spring Is." She uses another technique for creating movement that you could try. [I show Kamara the poem, and read it aloud.]

KAMARA: The words go sideways . . .

CARL: Yeah, you see how the words move down the page? The words, they kinda move, just like they're going down the stairs, just like they're jumping off the plate, right?

KAMARA: [nods]

CARL: Poets will sometimes make words move down the page to create the feeling that there's movement in a poem. And that could be a technique you could try in your poem. Just have the words go like that because then your eyes have to move, just like the ball is moving. Why don't you try just writing that verse over on a different piece of paper, just to see what it looks like to do that.

KAMARA: But I'm not running down the stairs, though, I'm passing the ball.

CARL: Right. You're not running down the stairs, but there's movement in your poem when you pass the ball, so doing this would give you another way to create that feel.

KAMARA: [nods]

CARL: Okay, so just try it and see what it's like, and we'll talk in a little while about the difference between the two drafts, okay?

When Ms. Clark and I checked in with Kamara, we found she had tried running her words down the page like Bobbi Katz does. We also found that Kamara had come up with her own variation on the technique—she ran the letters of individual words down the page, too (see Figure 4–7). Kamara told us she liked this new technique better than slanting words because the words seemed to move faster, just like the way a basketball moves through the air when she passes one.

B A S K E T B A L L !

my first time playing

THE GAME

In front of an audience

CONFUSED

Are we playing offense
or deffense? Why am I
the only one at this end
of the court?

OK I got the ball so I'll
P
A
S
          S IT! The ball is
GOING
    GOING
        GOING
To the other team
I guess this is what
they mean by
          BAD PASSES!

FIGURE 4-7   Second draft of Kamara's "Basketball!"

This first challenge we face in this kind of a conference is to familiarize students with the text. I usually do this work after I give students critical feedback and before I teach. In my conference with Kamara, I read "Spring Is" aloud because the poem is a short one. In other conferences, when I match students up to longer texts, I ask them to read the texts independently and make an appointment to continue the conference after they've read the pieces, either later that period or the next day. If I try to read a long text aloud to students, or wait for them to read it, conferences will take too long.

In this kind of conference, it is also more likely we'll have to teach students by pointing out in the text what we want them to learn, instead of asking them to compare their writing to the model text. It's unreasonable, after all, to expect students to come to brilliant insights into how an author uses a craft technique a few seconds after we've read a text aloud, or right after they've read it for the first time. In my conference with Jennifer earlier in this chapter, one reason she realized so quickly she could show time passing in more places in her story is because her class had read and reread and analyzed *The Relatives Came*. While I thought Kamara did well to notice that "the words go sideways" in "Spring Is," she initially seemed to think that Katz wrote the poem that way only to look like stairs, not to create movement. I still had to explain to Kamara that Katz seemed to be doing both, and why.

When I introduce students to unfamiliar writing mentors, I go through the following steps:

- I familiarize students with the text by reading it aloud or by asking students to read the text independently.
- I point out the craft technique in the text.
- I ask students to speculate about why the author used the technique, or I explain what I know about the technique.
- I ask students to try the technique.

Assembling a Collection of Mentor Texts

Teachers often ask me, "Is there a list of mentor texts?" Once a classroom teacher myself, I know how little time there is to search for texts, and so I tell them I'm amenable to sharing whatever titles are currently on my list. (I include a bibliography of mentor texts in the Appendix.)

However, when I give them my list, I caution teachers that the texts I've used successfully in conferences with students may not work as well—or at all—with theirs. I tell them how dismayed I was when I moved from Kentucky, where I taught students in a rural town south of Louisville, to Illinois, where I taught students in a suburban school district north of Chicago, and found that my new students weren't interested in many of the texts I had spent so much time locating in Kentucky. I had to assemble an almost entirely new collection.

Ultimately, we each have to put together our own collection of mentor texts, one that meets our needs as teachers and the needs of the students we teach. When we put together our collections, we are faced with a number of challenges:

- We need strategies for finding texts.
- We need criteria for deciding which texts will be useful teaching tools.
- We need criteria for assessing whether or not our collection of texts is varied enough to help us in many different conferences.
- We need strategies for getting our hands on texts at the exact moments we need them during conferences.

Searching for Mentor Texts

It's happened many times. I arrive at a school, and before I've even made it past the security guard, one of the teachers I'm working with dashes up and tells me she spent her whole Saturday at a bookstore and bought several hundred dollars worth of literature to use in her writing workshop. She insists I visit her classroom immediately, and on the way she breathlessly tells me about all the ways she's going to use the new books. The tall stack of books she has bought is indeed an impressive one, and I copy down the titles of several of her discoveries.

I've been moved by the commitment to their students and to the teaching of writing these teachers have demonstrated in their quests to find just the right mentor texts. At the same time, however, I know that not all of us have the time—or the cash—to do what these teachers have done. How, then, can we put together the collection of texts that we need for our writing conferences?

Most important, I've learned that we don't need hundreds of texts. It's easy to fall into the trap of believing that we do. I've seen lists circulated by district offices that list twenty books with great leads, twenty books with rich settings, fifteen books with wonderful endings, and so forth. We read these lists and feel a sense of panic because we have only one or two of the books in each category, and we haven't heard of many of the other titles. And when we go to the bookstore, some of them are out of print.

While I think that these lists are excellent resources, and their creators are well-intentioned, I think that lists that categorize the texts by a single craft issue lead us to think that each one is "good for" teaching only one thing. In my experience, though, there are many, many ways that a single well-written text can be used to teach students in conferences.

I learned this lesson several years ago from Katie Wood Ray, who was then a staff developer for the Reading and Writing Project, when I took her course on craft at the Project's Summer Institute. When Katie conferred with me, I was impressed by how she pulled just the right text out of her bag—Sandra Cisneros's *The House on Mango Street*—to help me get a clearer image of what I was trying to do in my piece. Intrigued by her obvious knowledge of literature and how to use it in her teaching, I spied on Katie as she conferred with several other students. I was amazed that in conference after conference, she used *The House on Mango Street*—but each time for a different purpose.

In each of my two collections of mentor texts—one for primary grades and one for upper grades—I have about twenty-five texts. That's it. In the collection I use in the primary grades, I have picture books and short texts: a couple of memoirs, a few list books, several number and alphabet books, and some nonfiction books. I have one good anthology of poems. In my upper-grade collection, I have four or five memoirs and the same number of short stories. I have several picture books. I have a few editorials and nonfiction feature articles. And I have one good anthology of poetry.

I realize it can be daunting for someone who is trying for the first time to assemble a collection of mentor texts to choose even twenty-five titles. Luckily, there are several ways to identify worthy candidates.

Consider Texts We've Already Read to Students   Any text we've read already with our students is a possibility. A poem we read to the class on the first day of school. A short story we featured as one of our read-alouds. Even a feature article we read to the students during Science or Social Studies could be worthy of our consideration.

Cast a Wide Net   We might find a good mentor text in any book or newspaper or magazine that we read, inside or outside of school. I've clipped editorials and letters to the editor from the newspaper in every city in which I've lived. I've cut album reviews out of *Rolling Stone* magazine. I've downloaded poetry from the Internet written by students who live halfway across the country. Today I find mentor texts for primary students in the big basket of books my wife and I have gathered for our daughter, Anzia.

Cut Excerpts from Longer Works   Parts of some texts stand alone very nicely. While I wouldn't expect a first-grade writer to be able to write the amount of text contained in Cynthia Rylant's picture book *When I Was Young in the Mountains,* I nonetheless have used the first page in conferences with first graders. In just two sentences—and by using just a single, telling detail—Rylant evokes an unforgettable image of her relationship to her grandfather, something many first graders can approximate. Likewise, with upper-grade children, I excerpt sections from Eloise Greenfield and Lessie Little's *Childtimes,* and I cut out parts of chapters in Jean Little's *Little By Little* that are self-contained memories comprised of a few scenes.

Use Student Writing   This is one source I wish I had taken more advantage of when I was a classroom teacher. Without fail, when I showed a student's piece in a mini-lesson, the interest level in the class rose exponentially. Why didn't I think to use those pieces in conferences, too? We might also use some of the "benchmark papers" given as examples of high-quality student writing in state or national assessments of writing. Using these texts has the added bonus of allowing us to integrate preparation for such writing tests into our day-to-day workshop teaching.

Involve Kids in the Hunt   As part of their reading lives outside of school, some of our students read the kinds of texts they're also making in writing workshop. Why not tell our students about the types of pieces we're trying to find? When I taught in Illinois, for example, it was my students who pointed me toward the *Chicago Tribune*'s Tuesday kids' section, where I found examples of the sorts of feature articles they found interesting. I still use some of the articles I found in the *Tribune* today.

Enlist the Aid of Our Colleagues   Let's assume we all can name five texts we could use in conferences. Imagine how our repertoire of texts would grow if we got together with our colleagues and shared our lists. This is exactly how teachers at Lakeside School in Merrick, Long Island, put together an impressive collection of mentor texts in just a few months. One group of fourth-grade teachers, for example, met once a month to share the titles of pieces they discovered and imagined the kinds of mini-lessons and conferences in which they could use the pieces.

Ask the School Librarian for Help   I've worked with several teachers who have enlisted the aid of school librarians in their searches. Such common sense! In many schools, the librarian is often an expert on children's literature. If we let librarians know what we're looking for, they not only might be able to find a few good pieces right away, but could pass others our way whenever they come across them.

Write Texts Ourselves   I often write pieces to use as mentor texts. When my Kentucky eighth graders were studying memoir, for example, I wrote one about my seventh-grade girlfriend. In my conferences during that genre study, I used the writing of Roald Dahl, Jean Little—and my own. And in Illinois, when I couldn't find any examples of the literature reviews my students were required to write for their science fair projects, I composed one myself.

Assessing a Text

Once we've identified a text as one we might want to use with students, we need to look at it very, very carefully. If we put it into our collection, we and our students are going to live with it for weeks, months, maybe even the whole school year. We're going to reread the text and count on it to spark discussions about craft. We're going to refer to it in minilessons. And, of course, we're going to talk about the text in numerous conferences.

A good mentor text is one that has affected students—and us. Maybe the text is a memoir or poem that made us laugh, or left us in stunned silence after we read the last line. Or maybe the text is an argument that angered us, or made us nod our heads up and down in agreement. It's these texts that students are most interested in revisiting. They want to figure out what the authors did to evoke such strong reactions so they can do the same to cause similar responses in their own readers.

A good mentor text should also be well-crafted. We should be able to imagine using the text in several different kinds of craft conferences. For example, I've used Donald Crews' picture book *Shortcut* to teach children in the primary grades how to write dialogue and how to make sound words get "louder" by capitalizing the letters. I've used Jean Little's "Maybe a Fight" (from *Hey World, Here I Am*) to teach upper-grade students how to get inside characters' heads and weave dialogue and narration together to write scenes.

Finally, a good mentor text is one that students in the class can emulate. That is, they can reasonably be expected to write pieces that are as long or as complex as the text. One of the reasons I use Nick Butterworth's *My Dad Is Awesome* or Jamie Lee Curtis's *When I Was Little* in conferences with first graders is simply because there is only one sentence on most pages. For some first-grade writers, this is plenty of text to write. And one of the reasons Cynthia Rylant's *When I Was Young in the Mountains* and Eric Carle's *The Very Quiet Cricket* are such effective texts to use with younger children is because children readily see and hear the repetition these authors use, and can immediately use the technique in their own picture books.

Length and complexity are also issues in upper-grade classrooms. I've worked with eighth graders who said to me, "I can't write that," when they looked at the short stories I showed them in conferences. When I took a hard look at the texts —stories containing as many as thirty or forty scenes—I had to agree with them. It would have been more reasonable for me to show them a short story like Cynthia Rylant's "Spaghetti" (from *Every Living Thing*), which contains only a couple of scenes.

Assessing a Collection of Mentor Texts
Just like a good diet includes a variety of foods, a useful collection of conferring texts should include different kinds of texts. These texts must, after all, meet the needs of the diverse writers in our classrooms.

First, our collections of mentor texts should reflect the voices and experiences of the children in our classrooms. It's vital that students in our classrooms hear familiar voices in some of the pieces we read to them. Even though craft can be studied independent of content, children often respond with more interest to stories about people with whom they can identify, and they are more likely to consider the authors of these stories as writing mentors. When I work in New York City classrooms, I make sure I have texts by authors such as Sandra Cisneros, whose voice grew out of an urban childhood that students can readily identify with. Many New York City students have gotten ideas from Cisneros of how to write about their own experiences growing up in a tough city environment.

A collection of mentor texts should also include a variety of genres. I've tried hard to collect examples of just about every kind of writing I've seen students make in writing workshop. I have memoirs, poetry, short stories, picture books, editorials, nonfiction feature articles, letters to the editor, and a few other genres ready to match up to students whenever the need for them arises. I even have a review of some of the latest video games to help the occasional student who insists on writing about them!

Finally, the mentor texts in our collections should be crafted in different ways. I've been struck by how little variety there is in many students' writing with regards to structure (I've read thousands of bed-to-bed pieces), sentence variety, and word choice. From talking with students, I've realized that many of them just don't know there are other ways to organize a piece or write a sentence. Consequently, my collection of mentor texts includes texts structured in several different ways. In my upper-grade collection, for example, I have Sandra Cisneros's "Papa Who Wakes Up Tired in the Dark" (from *House on Mango Street*), which focuses on a single event, and Eloise Greenfield and Lessie Little's "Yer Fella" (from *Childtimes*), which includes several events separated by years of time. It's also important that we include authors who do a variety of things with sentences and words. Cynthia Rylant, for example, juxtaposes lengthy sentences with short ones in *The Relatives Came*. And I marvel at the way Sandra Cisneros picks just the right words to evoke the childhood world of her characters in "Eleven" (from *Woman Hollering Creek*).

How to Keep Mentor Texts at Our Fingertips
Many fans of the television show "Star Trek" have seen the infamous "blooper reel," which is a compilation of humorous mistakes made by the actors during filming. Since schools often videotape my conferences—and not every one of those conferences is one I'm proud of—I've often thought I should put together my own personal blooper reel.

During one of these videotaped conferences, I tell a third grader I have the perfect memoir to help her with the ending she is writing. The camera catches me fishing around in my carry bag for several minutes, ultimately coming up empty-handed. I ask the teachers if they have a copy of the memoir, but each of them shakes her head. Finally, I look right into the camera lens and shrug.

We want to make sure moments like this don't happen. There are several ways to ensure we (almost always) have the right mentor texts at our fingertips when we need them.

Give Students Copies of Mentor Texts   It's a good idea to give students copies of texts the class has read and studied. Then, during conferences, we can ask them to bring out their copy of the piece we want to discuss with them. Isoke Nia, one of my colleagues at the Reading and Writing Project, has a wonderful name for these handouts: "literary gifts." When I pass out literary gifts, I ask students to put them into their writing folders or to tape them onto a page in their writers notebooks.

Put Copies of Texts Where We Can Easily Get to Them   Many schools lack the copy budget to allow us to make copies of model texts for all our students (and in some cases, copyright issues forbid us to do so). When this is the case, we can make a few bound sets of student texts (or write for permission to duplicate copyrighted material) and put them in the classroom library, the writing materials center, or in baskets on each table in the classroom. Or instead of binding the texts, we can laminate a few copies of each one.

Carry Copies of Texts With Us When We Confer   I take copies of texts I'll probably need in conferences that day and tuck them under the record-keeping forms on my clipboard. Usually, I have a few copies of each text. I put a big Post-it note on the last copy of each text to remind myself not to give it away before making more copies.

How Do I Develop a Knowledge Base About Craft?
When I give workshops on conferring, teachers tell me that they are anxious about teaching students how to learn from writing mentors. "I'm not comfortable with the idea of using literature in conferences," they say. "I didn't learn that much about the craft of writing when I was in school. How do I go about learning more?"

In response, I say that over the years I've acquired—and continue to acquire—my knowledge about craft and how to teach students about craft from several sources. I draw upon all of this knowledge in conferences.

From Professional Books
There are several indispensable professional books that offer in-depth discussions of the craft of writing. William Zinsser's *On Writing Well* (1980), Ralph Fletcher's *What a Writer Needs* (1993), and Don Murray's *Write to Learn* (1998) are the three I've relied on most as a classroom teacher and staff developer.

Several books offer guidance on how to teach students to craft their writing. A professional library would be incomplete without Katie Wood Ray's *Wondrous Words* (1999), a book that discusses the whole-class and one-to-one work of teaching students how to study craft. In Ralph Fletcher and JoAnn Portalupi's *Craft Lessons* (1998), the authors describe numerous craft mini-lessons, by grade level. My knowledge of the craft of poetry has been deepened by reading and rereading Georgia Heard's *For the Good of the Earth and Sun* (1989) and *Awakening the Heart* (1998). Shelley Harwayne's *Lasting Impressions* (1992) and Barry Lane's *After the End* (1993) are also rich sources of information about teaching craft.

From Our Own Writing

Ever since I began teaching students about craft, the experience of writing has felt different to me. As I write, I'm very conscious of how I craft my writing. What I learn from spying on myself as I write has given me ideas of what to teach students about craft. And I am reminded time and again of how hard it is to craft my writing, something that's good to keep in mind when I'm working with students.

From Reading with a Writer's Eye

As I read with my "writer's eye," I get lots of ideas for craft mini-lessons. No matter whether I'm reading a championship game preview in *The New York Times* sports section or an editorial in *The Nation* magazine or a poem on the wall of a New York City subway car, I can't help but notice how one writer repeated a phrase over and over or another writer used metaphor or how yet another connected several phrases together with the word *or*. Sometimes I know the name for what I am noticing, and sometimes I don't. Either way, what I notice when I read gives me ideas of things I can try in my own writing—and ultimately of things I can suggest that students try in their writing.

IN CONFERENCES, WE help students learn lessons about craft from writing mentors. We want them to have the same kinds of relationships with writers that I developed with Ralph Fletcher as I wrote this book.

In some conferences, we nurture preexisting relationships between students and their writing mentors. Our job in these conferences is to help students learn more from their mentors by revisiting their mentors' texts, studying them further, and then trying out what they notice in their own writing.

In other conferences, we introduce students to writing mentors. In these conferences, we familiarize students with texts, use the texts to teach them, and then nudge them to try out what we've taught.

In order to teach students how to learn from writing mentors, we need to assemble a collection of mentor texts to have at our fingertips when we confer. As we put together our collection, we need to consider our needs as teachers as well as the needs of the students we teach.

References

Butterworth, Nick. 1989. *My Dad Is Awesome*. Cambridge, Massachusetts: Candlewick Press.

Carle, Eric. 1990. *The Very Quiet Cricket*. New York: Philomel.

Cisneros, Sandra. 1984. *The House on Mango Street*. New York: Vintage Books.

————. 1991. *Woman Hollering Creek*. New York: Vintage Books.

Crews, Donald. 1992. *Shortcut*. New York: Scholastic.

Curtis, Jamie Lee. 1993. *When I Was Little*. New York: HarperCollins.

Fletcher, Ralph. 1993. *What a Writer Needs*. Portsmouth, NH: Heinemann.

————. 1995. *Fig Pudding*. New York: Clarion.

Fletcher, Ralph, and JoAnn Portalupi. 1998. *Craft Lessons: Teaching Writing K–8*. York, ME: Stenhouse.

Greenfield, Eloise. 1978. *Honey I Love and Other Love Poems*. New York: Harper.

Greenfield, Eloise, and Lessie Jones Little. 1979. *Childtimes: A Three-Generation Memoir*. New York: Crowell.

Harwayne, Shelley. 1992. *Lasting Impressions*. Portsmouth, NH: Heinemann.

Heard, Georgia. 1989. *For the Good of the Earth and Sun*. Portsmouth, NH. Heinemann.

————. 1998. *Awakening the Heart*. Portsmouth, NH: Heinemann.

Hopkins, Lee Bennett, ed. 1992. *Pterodactyls and Pizza*. New York: Trumpet Club.

Lane, Barry. 1993. *After the End*. Portsmouth, NH: Heinemann.

Little, Jean. 1987. *Little by Little: A Writer's Education*. New York: Viking.

————. 1986. *Hey World, Here I Am*. New York: Harper.

Murray, Donald. 1998. *Write to Learn*. New York: Harcourt Brace.

Ray, Katie Wood. 1999. *Wondrous Words: Writers and Writing in the Elementary Classroom*. Urbana, Illinois: NCTE.

Rylant, Cynthia. 1982. *When I Was Young in the Mountains*. New York: Dutton.

————. 1985. *Every Living Thing*. Scarsdale, NY: Bradbury.

————. 1985. *The Relatives Came*. Scarsdale, NY: Bradbury.

Zinsser, William. 1980. *On Writing Well*. New York: Harper.

5 Laying the Groundwork for Conferences

Mini-Lessons

At 6:54 this morning, when I peeked into my daughter's room, I saw she had just woken up and was staring at the bird mobile that hangs over her bed. When Anzia realized I was standing in the doorway, she sat up and said, "Da-da . . . read." And so for the next half hour, we read several books, some of them three or four times. Not a bad way to start a Saturday.

My wife, Robin, and I are impressed that at nineteen months, Anzia loves books and wants to be read to constantly. But we aren't surprised. After all, we've been laying the groundwork for two years. We started to put together our collection of children's books even before she was born. Very few days have gone by in her life when we haven't snuggled up together several times with a pile of books. We read with Anzia everywhere—at home, on long car or airplane rides, even on subway trips into Manhattan. And Anzia's days always end with readings of *Goodnight Moon* or *Guess How Much I Love You* or *Goodnight Gorilla*.

During workshops, when I show videotapes of my conferences, I can tell from teachers' expressions and comments that they are impressed with the writing work they see students doing. After the workshops, some of the teachers approach me and say, "I appreciate all that you said today about conferring with students about their work, but what I want to know is how these students learned to do all of this work in the first place."

When a student tells us, "Well, I'm revising 'My Sleepover,'" as Becky did in Chapter 2, we are hearing the results of weeks, months, even years of groundwork laid by her current teacher and teachers who taught her in previous years. The place we lay much of this groundwork is in mini-lessons, the short whole-class lessons (between five and fifteen minutes) most teachers give at the beginning of each day's writing workshop.

We give mini-lessons because we feel that many of the students in our classes need to learn about a strategy or writing technique in order to become better writers. In *The Art of Teaching Writing*, Lucy Calkins

(New Edition, 1994) explains how important it is that our decisions about what to teach in mini-lessons are based on our assessment of students' needs as writers:

> Although mini-lessons may often look like miniature speeches, like brief lectures, they are entirely different from the lectures that were such a part of my own schooling. The difference can be summed up in a single word: *context*. In mini-lessons, we teach *into* our students' intentions. Our students are first deeply engaged in their self-sponsored work, and then we bring them together to learn what they need to know in order to do that work. This way, they stand a chance of being active meaning-makers, even during this bit of formal instruction. First our students are engaged in their own important work. Then we ask ourselves, "What is the one thing I can suggest or demonstrate that might help the most?" (93–94)

Many students develop their agendas for their writing directly in response to our whole-class teaching. Mini-lessons give us opportunities not only to give students information about different kinds of writing work, but to persuade students to adopt our agendas for them as writers as their own, and equip them to try out what we teach in their independent writing. Students learn what we've taught *after* the mini-lesson, when they try out what we've taught in their own writing. Mini-lessons are effective, then, only when we inspire and enable students to try out what we've taught.

Effective mini-lessons have an enormous impact on conferences. When we confer with students who are doing work sparked by today's mini-lesson, or one we gave last week or a month ago, we can spend our time helping them extend and deepen the work they're already doing. We don't have to spend as much of our conference time teaching students about new kinds of writing work, because we've already done that teaching in mini-lessons. Nor do we have to expend our energy in conferences nudging many students to try out work for the first time, because our mini-lessons already provided that nudge for them.

In this chapter, I discuss how we can give mini-lessons that lay the groundwork for conferences in which we extend and deepen work students are already doing. I also offer some advice about how to keep mini-lessons truly "mini" so that they don't eat up precious time that students need for writing and learning, and that we need for conferring. Finally, I discuss the share session, the whole-class meeting at the end of the writing workshop in which we follow up on what we taught in that day's mini-lesson.

The Architecture of Effective Mini-Lessons

My colleagues and I at the Teachers College Reading and Writing Project have noticed that workshop teachers who give effective mini-lessons plan not only what they are going to teach, but how they are going to teach in a mini-lesson.* Their mini-lessons, in fact, have a predictable "architecture" to them (see Figure 5–1). That is, while the content of their mini-lessons changes from day to day, the way that they structure the lessons remains constant. Within this predictable architecture, we noticed that teachers have parts of their mini-lessons in which they teach students, encourage students to try what they've taught in their writing, and equip them to do so.

A Close Look at One Mini-Lesson

Norma Chevere's fifth graders at P.S. 155 in East Harlem were in the midst of a genre study of poetry. When I arrived one afternoon in her classroom, Norma told me that during the past several days, students had been having some difficulty with finding ideas for poems, and she asked if I could address this issue in a mini-lesson. I sat down in the authors chair in the meeting area—the signal for students to gather—and a minute later, Norma's thirty-six students had arranged themselves in front of me on the classroom rug.

I began the mini-lesson with the connection. I shared Mrs. Chevere's assessment with the students, and told them what I was going to teach that day.

> Mrs. Chevere told me that you've been busy studying poetry and writing poems during the past week. She's also told me that many of you have been having trouble finding ideas for new poems. So what I want to talk about today is how you can find ideas for poems in entries in your writers notebooks, and how you can use those entries to write poems.

My connection made, I began to teach. In the second part of the mini-lesson, I gave students information about using their notebooks to

---

*The thinking in this chapter originated in a study group on mini-lessons that Teresa Caccavale, Lucy Calkins, Grace Chough, Mina Chudasama, Isoke Nia, and I had the good fortune to be part of during Thursday think-tank meetings of the Teachers College Reading and Writing Project.

THE ARCHITECTURE OF A MINI-LESSON

- A mini-lesson begins with a *connection* in which we tell students what we will be teaching them, and why.
- Next, we *teach* students about a kind of writing work, either by giving them information or by helping them gather information about that work.
- After we teach, we often have students *have-a-go* with the work we've taught them—that is, they give the work a brief try.
- Finally, we end the mini-lesson by *linking* the lesson to students' independent writing.

FIGURE 5–1   The architecture of a mini-lesson

find ideas for poems by demonstrating the strategy right in front of them.

> My notebook is like a mine. When I reread all the entries I've made in it, I see all this rough stuff, but it all has a lot of potential. Some of the entries, in fact, have the potential to be good poems. Sometimes when I reread I find entries that already feel like poems—there's something about the way I wrote the words. Sometimes as I reread there's a feel-

ing behind an entry that tells me it could be a poem. It doesn't look like a poem, or sound like a poem, but that feeling reminds me of one I've had when I've read poetry.

What I'm going to do now is show you what I do once I've found an entry in my notebook that feels like it could become a poem. As you were coming to the meeting area, I found one of these entries, and I'm actually going to start writing a poem off of it in front of you. It's an entry about the homeless people in my neighborhood. (I read.)

> They come in shifts each day: the lady who sits cross-legged on the corner; the couple; and the guy who stands and smiles. I can only name them by how they look, not with names, these homeless people. The cross-legged lady always sits on the corner, her empty cup protected by her lap, held by both of her hands. She raises the cup to me when I pass, like it is she who is offering me something, instead of like she who is wanting something. The cross-legged lady does not speak with her mouth; her eyes, sunken into tired skin, plead with me to help her out . . .

When I was flipping through my notebook before and saw this entry, it kind of felt like a poem already—it's not a poem right now, it doesn't look like a poem, does it? [I hold up the page of the notebook for the students to see. They shake their heads.] When I read it, though, the entry had feelings in it, sad and lonely feelings, and those are the kind of feelings I explore by writing poems.

So I'm going to start a poem right now, right here on this piece of chart paper. Let's see how I can start this. One of the lines I like in the entry is the one about sitting on the corner, so I think I'll start with that. [I write, *On the corner she sits,* as my first line.] Let's see, what feels like it could come next? I'm thinking about what I wrote in that entry. [I look at the chart paper and reread what I wrote aloud, then I write a new line, *Her cup in her lap.*] Let's see, what next . . . What really strikes me is how she raises the cup when I pass her by, like this. [I use my hands to show the students how the lady raises the cup]. It's like the way she raises the cup to me, the cup is a very special thing, it is very hard to describe . . . It's like the way she holds the cup is the way someone in church would hold something special . . . [I reread what I've written and add on, *She raises the cup to me, The cup is a holy thing.*] I'm going to play with the image of the cup being holy. You know how in church you're offered communion if you're Catholic . . . It's almost like when the priest raises the cup to you when you take Communion, it feels like the lady is offering me something like that . . . [I reread the poem aloud and add, *She's offering me a New York City communion.*]

   I'm not going to go any further with this right now. I want to point out a few things about what just happened. You recognize some of my entry in this poem, don't you? The beginning of the poem is similar to what's in my notebook, but then I came up with ideas that weren't in my notebook, this part about the cup being holy and this one about the New York City communion. I want you to see that I didn't just copy over my entry and make it look like a poem. I started to play with what was in my notebook, and different images came into my head. The poem evolved as I was drafting.

I was finished with my teaching, but not my mini-lesson. I still needed to equip students to try out what I had just taught in their independent writing. In the third part of my mini-lesson—the have-a-go—I asked the class to look in their notebooks for entries that could become poems.

   What I'd like all of you to do right now for a few minutes is flip through your notebooks and see if you can find an entry you can imagine turning into a poem. If you find one, fold over the corner of the page to help you remember where it is. That way, if you're trying to come up with an idea today—or three days from now—you can fall back on the entry to get you started. [The students spend several minutes reading through their notebooks. Many of them fold over the corners of several pages.]

Finally, in the fourth part of the mini-lesson, I linked the lesson to students' independent writing. I asked which students thought they would use the strategy during that day's workshop.

   Who is starting a new poem today? [Twelve students raise their hands.] So there's a bunch of you. Which ones of you would be willing to use an entry in your notebook to launch a new poem? [Ten of the students with their hands raised keep them raised.] I can't wait to find out what happens to you when you use your notebook to launch new poems. When we come back to share today, I'll be sure to make those of you who try this famous [that is, recognize them in that day's share session]. Are you all ready to get to work? Let's go.

Mrs. Chevere and I were able to assess the effectiveness of this mini-lesson during the rest of the workshop. Of the four conferences we had with students, two of them were with students who were using notebook entries to write poems. When the class gathered for the share session at the end of the workshop, we asked the students how many of them had used the strategy. Twelve of them raised their hands, or one-third of the class. (Most of the other students in the class had spent the period working on drafts of poems that were already in progress, and had not needed a strategy for finding ideas for new poems.) And when I returned to Norma's class the next week, she told me that students were continuing to use their notebooks to help them find new ideas for poems.

The First Component of an Effective Mini-Lesson: The Connection

In the first part of the mini-lesson, we let students know what we've noticed about them as writers, and what we're going to teach them to help them be better writers. We call this part *the connection* because in this part we let students know how our teaching is connected to their needs as writers.

We often begin the connection by explaining why we're giving the mini-lesson. We might say, "After writing workshop yesterday, I was reading your writing and I noticed . . ." or "In conferences yesterday, I saw that you were having trouble with . . ." When we explain to students what we've been noticing about them as writers, we are letting them know that what we are going to teach them was designed with their specific needs in mind. We are giving them a personal stake in the lesson that follows, a reason to make what we talk about part of their agendas.

In the connection, we also tell students what we will teach them. We might say, "So today I'm going to teach you . . ." or, "What I want to talk with you about is . . ." The connection, then, helps students know what to listen for in the talk that follows—and, by giving it a name, helps them hold on to it in their minds after the mini-lesson is over.

The Second Component of an Effective Mini-Lesson: We Teach

In the second part of the mini-lesson, we teach, either by giving students information, or by helping them gather information about a kind of writing work.

As we plan for a mini-lesson, then, we must decide whether the lesson will be one in which we give or help students gather information. And once we've made that decision, we must decide which one of several methods for giving or gathering information we will use.

Teaching by Giving Information

When we teach by giving information, we give the students a short talk about a kind of writing work. There are several methods we can use to give information.

Give an Explanation Sometimes we teach by describing the writing work we want students to learn. For example, if we were teaching students about how to reenter a draft and get words flowing again, we might say, "When writers go back to their writing—when they start up each day, after they've been interrupted in the middle of writing, or if they've gotten stuck—they often reread what they last wrote as a way of getting words to flow again. As they reread, the words they've already written help them think of new ideas, and more words start to form in their minds. Then they pick up their pencils or pens, or start typing on their keyboards, and they're off again."

We often begin our explanations by telling students that the work we're going to describe is something that writers do. This kind of "name dropping" inspires some students to try the work in their writing. We might say:

- Something I do when I'm writing is . . .
- I want to tell you about something that I read Mildred Taylor does when she writes.
- The work I want to discuss with you is something that writers do.

Show Examples We can give students information about a kind of writing work by showing them a mentor text in which the author did this work. If we want students to see how writers transition from one part of a story to another, for example, we might use an overhead projector to project a piece on a screen, and then point out the transitions. Or if we want students to get ideas for the kinds of entries they can write in their writers notebooks, we might read them some of what we've written in ours.

Demonstrate   Probably the most powerful way we can give students information about how to do a kind of writing work—and persuade them that it's worth their time to try out that work—is for us to demonstrate that work in front of them. When we demonstrate, after all, we show students what a writer *actually does* while doing a kind of writing work—and since we want our students to actually do this work themselves, this kind of information is essential. When I used an entry in my writers notebook to help me get started with a poem in Norma Chevere's class, for example, I showed her students how I pick a line from an entry to get started with a poem, how I constantly reread what I've already written, and how I use my hands to help me come up with images. And I showed the students that poems don't pop out of writers' heads fully formed; to the contrary, writing a poem can be a slow, halting process.

Use a Fishbowl   When we want to give students information about how they can have effective peer conferences (or response groups), we can have students "fishbowl" a conference in front of the rest of the class. As the students confer, we might caption what they do—that is, give names to the moves they make in their conversation. For example, when one of the students in the fishbowl says, "I really need help with my ending," we might say to the class, "Tanya just set an agenda for this peer conference." Sometimes we're part of the fishbowl, stopping at various points to say, "See what I just did?" or "See what Tanya just did?" And in some fishbowls, we might stop the students in the middle of their conversation and teach them how to improve the conference.

Teaching by Gathering Information
When we teach by gathering information, we lead the class in a discussion in which students put together information about a kind of writing work themselves. As facilitators of the discussion, we have several responsibilities. First, we initiate the discussion. We might say, "I'd like for us to have a talk about the different strategies you use to find ideas to write about in your writers notebook," or "I want for us to take a look at several leads today, and have you name some of the different ways that writers begin their pieces."

As students talk, we facilitate the discussion. We might ask students to clarify what they say by asking, "I'm not sure I understand what you just said. Could you give it another try?" We might ask students to extend what they say by responding, "That's interesting. Could you say more about that?" And we might ask a student—or his class— to reconsider something he's said by saying, "I don't agree with what you just said about memoir. Is there a memoir we've read that led you to think that?" or, "Do we all agree with what Josh just said?" Finally, we make a record of what students say, on a piece of chart paper, the blackboard, or an overhead transparency. We might ask students, too, to take notes on the discussion in their writers notebooks.

In these discussions, we ask students to gather information from one of two sources.

From Their Experiences as Writers   In some discussions, we gather information by drawing upon students' experiences as individual writers. For example, let's say we want to teach students that there are numerous strategies for adding on to their texts. We know there are some students in our classes who add-on by using carets, others who use arrows, others who use footnotes, and so on. By saying to students, "I'd like to have a discussion today about the different strategies you use to add-on to your stories," we initiate a discussion in which students share their individual strategies. By the end of the discussion, the class will have assembled a list of strategies that is larger than most students' individual repertoires.

From Texts   In other discussions, we help students gather information by discussing texts. If, for example, we want students to understand the characteristics of the genre of feature articles, we might say to them, "During the past several days, we've read several feature articles. Today I'd like to discuss with you what you think a feature article is." At the end of this kind of discussion, we hope that the class will have come up with a list of the characteristics of feature articles that will help guide them as they write their own.

**The Third Component of an Effective Mini-Lesson:
The Have-A-Go**

In some mini-lessons, it makes sense for us to have students briefly try out what we've just taught them before we end the mini-lesson. The have-a-go usually lasts from two to four minutes.

It's important to note that the purpose of the have-a-go *isn't* for students to learn how to use the strategy or technique we taught. Its purpose is to enable students to try out the strategy or technique when they have an authentic need for it in their independent writing—when they'll have the time they need to learn how to use it. Giving a strategy or technique a brief try helps them remember what we've taught when they're ready to use it later that period, or several days later. And for many students, the have-a-go is the nudge they need to break through their resistance to trying new things in their writing.

There are several ways to structure the have-a-go.

Students Say Something to Neighboring Students
Sometimes we tell students to turn to a neighbor and use a variation on the "say something" strategy developed by Jerome Harste, Carolyn Burke, and Dorothy Watson (Short, Harste, with Burke 1996, 512–13). Instead of talking with a classmate about a text they've just read, students talk about what we just taught, and about how they might use it in their writing. This kind of talk gives students some time to process our teaching, and to make plans.

Students Look at Their Writing and Make Plans
Other times we ask students to look through their writers notebooks or at their drafts and imagine where in their writing they might be able to use what we taught. For a couple of minutes, students reread their writing and write a note or stick Post-its on places where they think it makes sense to try out what we taught.

Students Participate in a Writing Exercise
We will often ask students to try what we've taught as an exercise separate from their independent writing. If we give a demonstration of how to free-write, for example, we will probably ask our students to try the strategy for one or two minutes. Or if we show students a scene from a memoir and point out the way the author wrote dialogue, we could ask students to try writing a few lines of dialogue using that author's style. After a few minutes of writing, we might stop the class and ask students what it was like for them to use the strategy or technique. Or we might ask them to share their experience with the student sitting next to them.

The Fourth Component of an Effective Mini-Lesson: The Link to Students' Independent Writing
Where in the first part of the mini-lesson we told students how the strategy we were going to teach them that day was connected to their needs as writers, in the fourth and final part of the mini-lesson—the

"link"—we ask which students in the class will commit to using what we taught in their independent writing *that writing workshop period.*

It's crucial that I point out that I don't expect—or want—every student in a class to commit to doing what I talk about in any given mini-lesson. First, not every student in a class needs to learn what I teach in a mini-lesson. And second, since I want students to be the kind of writers who have their own plans for their writing, I expect that some students will have work that they think is more important to do than what I talked about in the mini-lesson during any given period. I hope these students will try what I talk about in a mini-lesson the next day, or the next week—and I let them know that's what I expect.

While I don't want every student in the class to commit to using what I teach in a mini-lesson, I do expect that many students will be willing to try out what I teach. It's simply unacceptable if no students, or just one or two, make the commitment. If students don't try out what I've taught, then they won't learn how to do the work. I also want to have conferences with students who are already trying the work, not just so I can extend and deepen their work, but so I can learn what I need to teach the whole class in follow-up mini-lessons.

There are several ways to get students to make a commitment during the link.

Ask for a Show of Hands

We can end the mini-lesson by saying, "Would you raise your hand if you think you can use what we talked about today in your work?" We might write down the names of the students who raise their hands on a piece of chart paper, the blackboard, or a clipboard, and tell the class that several of these students will report back to the class about their work during the share session at the end of the period.

Promise to Make Students Famous

Another way to end the mini-lesson is to tell students that we'll make some of them "famous"—that is, highlight their work in front of the class—for trying out what we taught. We might say, "During our share session today, I'll be sure to make those of you who try out this strategy today famous." Or we might tell them, "If you use this strategy this period, will you be sure to sign your name on this piece of chart paper so I can know to make you famous during share today?"

Suggest That Students Incorporate What We've Taught into Their Plans

During the past several years, many teachers in the Reading and Writing Project community have found it valuable to nurture ongoing relationships between students that they call "writing partnerships." If, at the end of mini-lessons, we have students talk briefly with their writing partners about their writing plans for that day's workshop, we might say, "As you meet with your writing partners today, tell them if you're going to try out the strategy we talked about."

Or we might have students jot down their plans for the period in an "assignment box" in their writers notebooks. We could say, "If you're going to do what we discussed today, be sure to put that in your assignment box."

Keeping Our Mini-Lessons Truly "Mini"

It's happened to all of us: we've glanced at the clock in the middle of a mini-lesson and noticed that we've been talking with the class for twenty or twenty-five minutes. Our mini-lesson has become a maxi-lesson. By the time we finish, our students have only ten, maybe fifteen, minutes left in the workshop period to write.

There *is* a lot to do in a mini-lesson. Still, most mini-lessons should take between five and ten minutes, with the occasional mini-lesson reaching fifteen minutes if it includes a discussion or if the students do a writing exercise. If, however, our mini-lessons take more time than this—and, consequently, take time away from students' independent writing—we defeat the purpose of the lessons. No matter how successful our mini-lessons may be in giving students information and persuading them to make what we've taught part of their writing agendas, they simply won't have the time they need to write and, through writing, learn how to do the work we've taught them. And we won't have much time to help them as they learn, either. Less time for students' independent writing, of course, means less time for conferring, too.

Once we've realized that we're giving maxi-lessons, we need to figure out why our whole-class teaching is taking up so much time. One or more of the following problems is usually the cause.

We Invite Too Much Student Talk

It's too easy to let students' comments take us way off course into directions we hadn't intended. For that reason, we have to decide in advance in which parts of our mini-lessons we're going to do the talking, and in which parts the students will—and then stick to our plan.

For example, when we are giving information, it's our job to do the talking, and the students' to observe and listen. To let students know what we expect of them, we might say, "I'm going to demonstrate how I read aloud my draft and look for errors. I want you to watch carefully as I do this—because I'm sure that many of you will want to try this yourselves today—but please don't say anything as I edit."

On the other hand, if we are gathering information, we'll want students to talk. We might say, "I'd like for us to have a talk about the different strategies you use to get your writing going again when you're stuck."

We Are Reading Pieces of Literature for the First Time

We don't have the time in a mini-lesson to read a piece of literature for the first time, give students a chance to respond to the piece as readers, and then use it to highlight a kind of writing work. Instead, we can read a piece we want to use in mini-lessons during another part of the day—for example, during read-aloud time. Or, instead of giving a mini-lesson or having a share session, we could read the piece, and then use that piece in our mini-lesson the next day.

We Give Many Examples When One or Two Will Do

In our excitement about showing students how to write dialogue leads or ambiguous endings, we pore through all of our favorite mentor texts and find five or ten examples—and then show each one to our students in a single jam-packed mini-lesson. Or as we demonstrate how we add-on to a draft, we get carried away and add-on to five or six places. After the second or third example, or the second or third add-on, however, students have gotten the point we're making. As we show them more, we lose their attention and they lose writing time. We can give students information by showing them one or two carefully chosen examples.

We Give Students Too Much Time for the Have-A-Go

Sometimes the have-a-go component of our mini-lesson stretches on for ten or fifteen minutes. We need to remember that the purpose of the have-a-go *isn't* for students to learn how to do the work we've just taught—it's simply to give the students a feel for doing the work. Three or four minutes is plenty of time for students to get a feel for many kinds of writing work, and to give them the confidence to use it in their writing.

We Repeat What We've Said Several Times

Sometimes at the end of the mini-lesson, we repeat what we've just taught because we're afraid that our students didn't get it. We have to remember that students don't get it because of the words we say. They get it when they try out what we've taught in their writing. As we teach a mini-lesson, it's our job to give the very best explanation we can, or help the students have the very best discussion they can have—but then we need to stop talking and give students the opportunity they need to write and learn.

We Don't Have All of Our Materials

Before we start a mini-lesson, it's essential that we have ready all the materials we're going to need. We have the overhead set up and plugged in so that we can show a copy of a text. Or we have a blank piece of chart paper on the easel and a magic marker in hand so we can copy down what the students say in a discussion. When, instead, we find ourselves saying, "Kids, hold on just a second so I can find a copy of *The Relatives Came*"—and we spend a few minutes searching for the text in the piles on our desk—we're taking time away from students' independent writing.

The Share Session

The share session, the short whole-class meeting (three to five minutes) that usually ends writing workshop, is another opportunity for whole-class instruction that helps lay the groundwork for conferences. What differentiates the share session from the mini-lesson is the purpose of the share, which is usually to follow up on what we talked about during that day's mini-lesson. During the share, students talk about and show the work they did during the period that was inspired by the mini-lesson. Their talk, not ours, is the heart of the share—talk is student-to-student, not teacher-to-student. Many students develop a deeper understanding of that day's mini-lesson after hearing their peers talk about their writing work. What their peers are doing as writers, after all, is either within their zone of proximal development or close to it.

Many teachers have students return to the meeting area for the share. We might call students to share by announcing, "Boys and girls, it's time for share." Or, as in Norma Chevere's room, we might signal students to stop writing and come and join us by sitting in the authors chair. Sometimes we might have students remain in their seats for the share session. Because we may be pressed for time—or because we don't have space for a meeting area—we might stop the class and say, "Let's stop our work now and have our share."

The point of the share session is for students to discuss the work they did as writers that period, *not* to read their pieces aloud from beginning to end. First graders might hold up their drafts to show their classmates how they used the strategies we demonstrated in the mini-lesson for adding information to the end of drafts. Students *might* read short parts of their pieces, if those parts are where they tried the strategy or technique we taught them. Fourth graders might read a few lines of dialogue from their short stories if we talked about writing dialogue in that day's lesson. In my middle school classes, when I gave mini-lessons on run-on sentences, students would write run-ons from their pieces on overhead transparencies, and then show their classmates how they punctuated them correctly.

In some share sessions, a single student will discuss the work she did that period. Often, we make a student with whom we had a conference earlier that period famous, because we want the class to hear about what she was doing or what we asked her to try in the conference.

In other shares, we might begin the meeting by asking the class, "So, who tried the work we talked about in the mini-lesson today?" We would then pick one or two of the students who raise their hands to talk about or show their work.

Occasionally, we might ask every student in the class to participate in a share. We could ask students to turn to the person next to them and talk about how they used what we taught in the mini-lesson that day— or, if they didn't try it, how they might use it the next day. Or we might conduct a "symphony share" in which every student reads one sentence from their piece. If we talked that day about word choice in the mini-lesson, we might say to the class, "I'd like for you to find a sentence in what you wrote today in which you used just the right words to get across what you were trying to say." Then students would read the sentences they chose.

Just like the mini-lesson, the share session is informational *and* persuasive. When students see that their classmates have tried what we talked about in mini-lessons, they are often inspired to try the same work. And, consequently, just like the mini-lesson, share sessions help us have conferences in which students are already doing new kinds of writing work, conferences that give us the chance to help them learn how to do that work even better.

THE MANY TIMES that my wife and I have sat next to Anzia with a picture book between us have been some of the most enjoyable moments we've spent together as a family. These experiences have taught Anzia that reading is a worthwhile activity, so much so that she asks to be read to several times a day. We are pleased that reading is part of Anzia's daily agenda.

The whole-class teaching we do in writing workshop gives us the opportunity to persuade students to make our agendas for them as writers their agendas. Our mini-lessons and share sessions, then, lay the groundwork for conferences in which we teach students how to deepen work they're already doing.

When we plan mini-lessons, we need to pay attention not only to the content of the lessons, but to how we organize them. While planning a lesson, it helps to think that mini-lessons have a predictable structure to them, or architecture. The components of a mini-lesson—the connection, the teaching, the have-a-go, and the link—are designed to teach students about a kind of writing work, encourage them to try the work in their independent writing, and equip them to do so.

References

Calkins, Lucy. 1994. *The Art of Teaching Writing.* Portsmouth, NH: Heinemann.

Short, Kathy G., and Jerome C. Harste with Carolyn Burke. 1996. *Creating Classrooms for Authors and Inquirers.* Portsmouth, NH: Heinemann.

Decisions, Decisions

Choreographing Conferences

6

Several months before my friend Mina got married, she looked at the pictures in my wedding album and sighed loudly. Finally, she said, "Your wedding was so simple. When Andre and I get married, it's going to be *such* a big production."

I chuckled when Mina described my wedding as "simple." It didn't really surprise me that she drew that conclusion. After all, Robin and I had our wedding ceremony atop Mill Ridge in the Blue Ridge Mountains of western North Carolina. The pictures show the two of us and the minister who married us standing under a homemade *chuppah*—a Jewish wedding canopy—adorned with wildflowers and ribbons. Surrounding us were some seventy relatives and friends, two of them sitting on folding chairs (the octogenarian-great aunts), the rest sitting in the grass or standing. All around us were mountains, and above us, a cloudless, deep blue sky.

Having one's wedding on a mountain ridge, however, is anything but simple. Robin and I faced all the challenges that everyone who gets married must face, and then some more. We had to find accommodations for seventy friends and relatives in a mountain hamlet so small that if you sneeze as you drive through, you miss it completely. At our wedding rehearsal, we discovered that the grass on Mill Ridge was chest high—consequently, we had to find friends willing to cut grass with scythes the next morning before the ceremony. And we had to figure out a way to safely transport those octogenarian great-aunts to the top of Mill Ridge, and then back down again. In other words, it required a great deal of thoughtful choreography for us to pull off our "simple" wedding in the Blue Ridge Mountains successfully.

Looking at pictures of teachers conferring with students, we could say, "I see teachers talking with students about their writing. It seems that conferring takes a lot less planning than teaching a lesson to an entire class." What we see in pictures of conferences, however, is deceptively simple.

It takes a lot of thoughtful choreography *before* we confer in order for conferences to go well. We make several decisions that have major impacts on the quality of the conversations we have with students. We must decide:

- Where should we conduct conferences?
- What tools do we need to help us confer?
- What do students need to have with them during conferences?
- At what point (or points) in the writing process should we confer with students?
- Who will initiate conferences?
- How much time should we devote to each conference?

Where Should We Confer?

The decision we make about where to confer with students—at our desks, their tables or desks, or at a special conference table—is one that influences students' willingness to talk with us, as well as the tone of our conversations with them.

When I confer, I choose to go to where students sit in the classroom. While conferences are not conversations between equals, students seem more at ease talking with me when I meet them where they feel most comfortable, at their desks or tables, even on the floor in a corner if that's where they're writing. By going to students to confer, we show them we are interested in talking with them about their writing. We all know from experience that conversations get off to a good start when one person expresses an interest in what the other has to say.

I don't recommend that we confer with students at our desks. Early on in my writing workshop experience, I found that calling students up to my desk put a damper on the conversations. My students seemed to freeze up the moment they arrived there, a natural response, after all, given that my desk was a symbol of my authority and power as a teacher.

I've visited several classrooms in which teachers have designated a special table as the "conference table." I believe the intention of these teachers was a good one: they wanted to create a neutral space where students would feel comfortable talking with them. But while the conference table felt like a neutral space to the teachers, I wasn't sure it felt that way to their students. The tables, after all, were often piled high with the teachers' stuff. And the way I often saw teachers alert a student that it was time to have a conference with him—by calling his name out in a loud voice—was no different than the way many teachers call students to their desks. Not surprisingly, many of the students seemed uncomfortable as they sat talking with their teachers.

Before I begin conferences, I sit down next to students so I can be at their eye level. I grab a nearby empty seat, or sit on one that I carry with me around the classroom. If a chair is unavailable, I kneel on the floor. The simple act of sitting down puts many students at ease and invites them to talk to us.

Sitting down next to students also helps us define our relationships with them. Were we to stand during a conference, we would literally be talking *down* to students. We all know that when we feel "talked down to" by another person, it's hard to enjoy a conversation with him. When we sit eye-to-eye with students, on the other hand, we talk *with* students about their writing.

As I'm sitting next to students, I speak in my "conference voice." That is, I make sure that I don't talk louder than the student with whom I'm conferring, or than any of the other students in the nearby vicinity who are talking with each other about their writing. And I work hard to make sure that the tone of my conference voice is a respectful one, and expresses an interest in the content of a student's writing, as well as the work he's doing as a writer.

These points may seem obvious, given that in conversations we usually match our partner's volume, and we try to be respectful and interested. One of the challenges of workshop teaching, however, is shifting back and forth from the whole-class voice we use when we talk in mini-lessons and share sessions to our conference voice, and it's helpful to think carefully about how we will talk in these different settings. And if we've been teaching in a traditional classroom in which we are used to lecturing our students for most of the day, it takes time and conscious effort to develop a conference voice.

What Tools Should We Bring With Us?

Many professionals have special tools that they carry with them as they do their jobs. Doctors drape stethoscopes around their necks. Mathematicians slide calculators into their pockets. Photographers sling cameras on their shoulders.

We writing teachers, too, need special tools to help us confer. As we make plans for our conferences, we should be thinking carefully about which tools we'll carry with us.

Record-Keeping Forms

Just like doctors keep records of their patients' visits, we need to keep records of conferences. These records help us keep track of when we conferred with students, what we talked about, and what we learned about students as writers.

Before I confer, I attach several record-keeping forms to a clipboard that I then carry with me as I go from student to student. As I talk with students during conferences, I jot down what we talk about. It took me a while to get used to listening and writing at the same time, but since I've developed this skill, my notes have become a much more accurate reflection of the conversations I have with students. There are still some conferences, however, where I need to take a minute after they're done to finish writing my notes.

Many of the teachers with whom I have worked have dismissed the need for record-keeping. "I want to concentrate on listening to my kids, not on taking notes," some explain. "I can keep all the details in my head," others say.

I nod when I hear these explanations. I used to say the same exact things myself, until a few embarrassing experiences persuaded me that keeping conference records was worth the effort.

For example, years ago I had a parent-teacher conference with Gregory's mother. She told me that Gregory enjoyed writing workshop but felt that I didn't like him very much. Puzzled, I asked her to explain why Gregory felt this way. I was mortified when she told me that Gregory had complained to her that I had writing conferences with many of his classmates, but never with him.

And Gregory wasn't the only student I had been overlooking. The next day, I passed out a piece of paper to every student in my class and asked them to write down how many conferences they had had with me since September. Out of thirty-seven children, five said that I hadn't conferred with them at all.

How had I failed to confer with these five students? Each of them, as it turns out, were quiet, independent students. In a large class filled with many needy children, I had inadvertently overlooked them.

After this experience, I began to keep records of when I conferred with each student. When I finished a conference, I recorded the date next to the student's name on a simple form I attached to a clipboard (see Figure 6–1). It was easy, then, to be sure I was conferring with all of my students. And it was a simple matter, too, to decide which students to confer with on any given day. After my mini-lessons, while the class was settling into their writing, I would scan this form and make plans to confer with students I hadn't talked to for several days.

Several months later, another embarrassing experience taught me the value of keeping track of what I talked about with students. I was conferring with Tiffany, who told me that she didn't have any ideas to

CONFERENCE RECORD — MARCH

STUDENT	DATES	
Tiffany A.	3/4	
Alisha	3/2	3/11
Terrence	3/2	3/9
Demeka	3/3	3/9
Frank	3/1	3/8
Gregory	3/3	
Doran	3/2	3/10
Kamara	3/5	
Jemel	3/1	3/8
Malika	3/4	3/10
Aida	3/5	
Tiffany G.	3/5	
Byron	3/5	3/10
Celeste	3/1	3/9
Jennifer	3/4	
Henry	3/2	3/8
Anibal	3/4	
Alex	3/3	3/11
Syeda	3/4	3/11
Chaylin	3/1	3/9
Meredith	3/8	
Edward	3/3	3/11
August	3/2	3/9

FIGURE 6–1   Conference record form

write about in her writers notebook that period. Consequently, I spent several minutes teaching her to "stretch a line"—that is, to reread an earlier entry in her writers notebook and find a line in that entry that sparked an idea for some new writing she could do.

When I finished, Tiffany asked, "Mr. Anderson, why did you teach me to stretch a line *again?*"

"What do you mean, 'again'?" I asked, puzzled.

"You taught me to stretch a line when you conferenced with me last week," Tiffany said. "Look." She flipped back several pages in her writers notebook and pointed to an entry. "I did the strategy here . . ." She turned a page. "And here." All around us, I could hear Tiffany's classmates giggling.

Because I had failed to remember what I had taught her in our previous conference, I wasted Tiffany's time and mine. So, I began to keep records of the content of the conversations I had with students about their writing.

I use a different form to help me keep track of what I talk about with students (see Figure 6–2). Since I only put four or five students' names on each form, there is enough space next to each student's name to take notes on two or three conferences. Depending on how large the class is, I may need six or seven of the forms.

I usually take notes on three areas of interest. First, I write down what I learn about a student as a writer: the work he is doing and insights I gain into who he is as a writer from what he says or from looking at his draft. Second, I record what I teach him in the conference. And, third, if I think the class might benefit from hearing what the student and I talked about during the conference, I jot down "Share" or "Mini-Lesson" to remind me at the end of the period to refer to our conference in that day's share session or to return to it when I plan the next day's mini-lesson. For example, Figure 6–3 shows the notes I took during the conference I had with Doran in Chapter 1.

The notes I take are only useful, of course, if I actually refer back to them. Consequently, before I meet with a student, I skim the notes from the last conference (or conferences). Not only does taking this time help me avoid the embarrassment of repeating what I taught the student in a previous conference, but it also helps me enter into the conference with lines of thinking in mind about a student. Let's say that when I met with Jordana a week and a half ago, we talked about how she might choose to write about her grandmother by focusing intensely on a single moment in time, just like Jean Little did in "Maybe a Fight" in *Hey World Here I Am*. After reading the notes of this conference, I

CONFERENCE NOTES

STUDENT	WRITING WORK	TEACHING MINI-LESSON?
Tiffany A.		
Alisha		
Terrence		
Demeka		

FIGURE 6–2   Conference notes form

STUDENT	WRITING WORK	TEACHING MINI-LESSON?
Doran	3/2 start ch.1 "Toy Prices" - logical plan, clear angle - model piece = "Bullies...", using it to craft lead	Looked at model piece to help him extend his concept of a non-fict lead ✓

FIGURE 6–3   Notes of conference with Doran

would be wondering if Jordana was able to pull this off, and about the kinds of revisions to the piece that I might need to help her make. During the conference, then, I would be listening for answers to these questions, or I might even ask them myself.

When I was a classroom teacher, once I filled up a set of these forms, I filed them. The forms were especially useful when I met with students to discuss their growth as writers—and their grades—when report cards went out. And they were equally useful to help me prepare for parent-teacher conferences.

Not everyone will like the forms I've just described. Some teachers don't like my record-keeping system because it only allows for recording a few conferences with each student. From talking with many teachers about their record-keeping systems, I've learned that each teacher needs to use forms that reflect their own individual needs, tastes, and personalities.

For example, Barbara Rosenblum, a second-grade teacher at P.S. 6 in Manhattan, uses just one form (see Figure 6–4) to record notes about her entire class. She divides a sheet of paper into squares, one for each student. By glancing at the sheet, Barbara can tell which students she hasn't seen in a few days—their squares are blank.

Many other teachers swear by this form. I've tried using it, but it just doesn't work for me. The squares are small, and as I'm conferring, I'm distracted by the fear that I'm going to run out of space. And it's only possible to take notes about one conference in a square.

Sarah-	Emily- 3/8- Found 3 ideas from rereading. Can't get started. Taught- make a list-choose 1.	Daniel- 3/13 Reread entry to find an idea. Taught- use strategy in other places. Found 3 more ideas	Nicole-	Sara-	Debbie-
Alex-	Larry-	Kate- 3/12-hiking with dad. Taught- write about 1 important thing, not all!	Sophie- 3/8-adding on to entry about getting hand stuck. Taught-find important part and stretch it.	Ira- 3/12-new entry, trying to use strong words. Named what he was doing, looked for other places	Lynn- 3/8 Taught strategy to revise: Reread draft, stop when you find a place to add thinking.
Joseph-	Alan- 3/13 Taught strategy for stretching a wondering. →Asking yourself questions about wondering-writing your thinking	Karen-	Max- 3/12-wondering about who owns parked bikes. Taught- writers sometimes make guesses in wondering	Jesse-	Gabrielle- 3/12-writing wondering about dog. Taught-stretch wondering by asking questions.
Alexa- writing about sister. Stuck for ideas. Taught- observe tonight to get new ideas	Holly- 3/8 Helped her make a plan for her picture book. Posted each page.	Paul- Spelling-identify parts of words that you know are correct/parts you know aren't	Sam-	Ben-	Harris-
Danielle-	Alexander-	Steven- 3/13 writing "all about" vacation. Taught- pick the important thing to write about.	Richard-	Barbara-	Mark- 3/12 couldn't get started. Taught- reread your notebook to get a new idea. Found 3 possibilities. Wrote a list.

FIGURE 6–4 Barbara Rosenblum's form

I've also seen teachers divide a notebook into sections, one for each student. In the front of the notebook, they have a page to record the dates they see each student, just as I described earlier. The advantage of keeping a notebook like this is that the notes for every conference with a child are all in one place. The disadvantage of this system—and the reason why it didn't work for me—is that it took a lot of flipping through pages to review the day's conferences when I was trying to make decisions about the next day's mini-lesson.

There will be advantages and disadvantages to every record-keeping system. Whether we use one of the systems I've described here, one we've read about elsewhere, or one we devise ourselves, the important thing is to choose a record-keeping system that allows us to keep track of who we talk with and what we talk about with them.

Literature

Imagine Bill Martin, Jr. or Katherine Paterson sitting next to you as you confer with students. You're talking with a first grader about organizing a picture book. And so you turn to Bill and say, "Maybe you could explain to Amelia how you put *Brown Bear, Brown Bear* together so she could get some ideas for how she might structure her picture book." Or you're talking with an eighth grader about developing a fictional character. So you ask, "Katherine, could you explain to Brad how you made Gilly come alive in *The Great Gilly Hopkins?*"

While we can't really have authors there in our classrooms to co-confer with us, we can do the next best thing: carry their poems and memoirs and essays around with us as we confer, especially the ones we've read recently with our class. As I discussed in Chapter 4, when we have these texts in hand with us when we confer, we can use them to teach students about many aspects of writing well. Together with students, we can look at texts and notice how the authors structured them or crafted the leads or made line breaks. These investigations can give students new images of what's possible in their writing.

We should also plan on carrying some of our own writing with us as we confer. When I teach students how to keep a writers notebook, for example, I bring my own writers notebook to conferences. When students are immersed in a memoir genre study, I attach a copy of a memoir I wrote to my clipboard. When I have my own writing with me, I can say to students, "You know, Lori, I collect a whole lot of different kinds of thinking in my notebook. Here, let me show you . . ." or "You're writing a background section for your feature article? Here, let me show you where I tried the same thing in mine." Students can just as easily get ideas for things to try in their writing from us as they can from authors who have won the Newbery Medal.

Post-it Notes

It frustrates me when students don't follow through and try what I've taught them in a conference. Some students have trouble remembering exactly what I've explained to them, especially if I confer with them at the end of the period and they aren't able to get back to their writing until that evening or the next day. Others don't follow through simply because they don't feel like it.

When I'm conferring with a student for whom follow-through is an issue, I'll jot down on a Post-it note what I want him to try in his writing and stick it in his writers notebook or on his draft. Those students who have forgotten what we talked about can jog their memories by reading the notes. And those who might not feel like following through have a visible reminder that I am expecting them to do so.

What Will Students Need to Have with Them?

The careful planning we do for conferences can be all for naught if students don't have all of their writing readily accessible. If, for example, Kawana has left her draft at home, we can't have a conference about her writing that day. Or if Steven can't find the first draft of his short story, we can't see the revisions he made to it before he wrote his second draft.

We have to decide what we want students to have with them at all times during writing workshop, and communicate our expectations to them. I suggest students have the following four things on their desks or tables:

- Their writers notebooks.
- Their most recent drafts.
- All previous drafts.
- Any piece of literature they as individuals or the class as a whole is using as a model.

Having their writing readily available saves us the time that students would otherwise take to fish through their desks or cubbies to find their first drafts or model pieces of literature. Separate from the fact that we might confer with a student, she should have these things on her workspace because she needs them to write.

Getting students into the habit of having these materials on their desks is part of the work we do during the first few weeks of school when we teach the children how the writing workshop operates. As part of a management mini-lesson, we tell students exactly what they should have out as they write. Then when we confer with students who have to locate their writers notebook or first draft in their desk, we tell them that their unpreparedness has wasted precious conferring time.

At What Point (or Points) in the Writing Process Should We Confer with Students?

Students need to get better at all aspects of writing if they're going to grow as writers. Thus, we have conferences while students are writing about ideas in their writers notebooks, drafting, revising, and editing.

This may seem like an obvious point. However, in reality many of us confer with students *after* they've finished revising and editing pieces, just before they publish. In these conferences, we make suggestions about what students can do to "fix up" their writing.

We have these "fix up" conferences for several reasons. They feel natural, given that when we were in high school and college, the only kind of response we received to our writing was after we turned in our papers. Although it feels more humane to tell students how to improve their final drafts than to cover their writing with red marks, in both cases our focus is on the writing, not the writers who composed the pieces.

Many of us have "fix up" conferences because we are uncomfortable when students publish flawed pieces. Even though we had a wonderful conference with a student about using dialogue—and his final draft shows the conference had a major impact on how he writes dialogue—when we see that his piece has a weak ending, we are dissatisfied. When we feel pressured by administrators or parents to make sure students' writing is flawless, we are especially susceptible to these feelings—and to the "fix up" conferences they engender.

We have to keep in mind that our goal in conferences is to help students become better writers. If we confer with a first grader about how to find a topic to write about, we've helped him become a better writer. Since many first graders spend just a day or two on pieces of writing, we probably won't confer with this student again about that piece. And it's bound to have several flaws. We have to make our peace with that inevitability. Even when we work with an older student, who may spend weeks on a single piece of writing, we are fortunate when we have two or three conferences with him during that time. As we confer with older students, we help them become better at several aspects of writing well, but not all. Their final pieces, too, will have flaws. It is part of our job to explain this to parents and administrators in a way that leaves them confident and supportive of our efforts.

It takes time, lots and lots of time, for students to become better writers. Over the course of the school year, as first-grade or eighth-grade students work on new pieces of writing, we'll have opportunities to confer with them about other kinds of writing work. Over the course of the school year we help students get better at all aspects of writing, not during the writing of a single piece.

Who Initiates Conferences?

One of the most basic decisions we have to make as we plan our conferences is who will initiate them. Will we? Will our students? Or will we both?

During my first few years in the classroom, I initiated almost every conference. After the mini-lesson, I took a minute to scan my conference records to see which students I hadn't conferred with for several days. During the period, I dropped in on these students unannounced and conferred with them.

One reason that I initiated conferences was because I wanted to confer with each student an equal number of times across the school year. If I had left it up to students to decide when they wanted to talk with me, then some would have wanted to see me every day, while others, quite honestly, would have chosen not to see me at all. Some of my students didn't ever seem to feel the need for conferences. And a number of my middle school students felt embarrassed when I talked with them in front of their peers.

I also didn't want to limit my conferences to when students were experiencing problems with their writing—the reason most cited when they asked for a conference. I didn't want students to become dependent on me to help them solve the problems they inevitably encountered. I was concerned that if students could ask for a conference whenever they ran into some difficulty, they would stop working until it was their turn. (In primary classrooms, students who want their teacher's help will sometimes form a line behind him as he moves around the room, a phenomenon I call "*Make Way for Ducklings* Syndrome.") Instead, I wanted students to develop a repertoire of strategies to use when they encountered difficulties, strategies such as peer conferring, recalling a mini-lesson, or studying a text written by a favorite author to see how that author solved the problem. Since I was the one who initiated most conferences, and since students didn't know when I would be conferring with them, my students learned to draw upon this repertoire of strategies when they ran into trouble.

I also wanted to confer with students when they *weren't* having trouble with their writing. Even when students felt that things were going well, I found there was still a lot I could teach them. For example, a second-grade student who is writing a "bed to bed" story about a day at camp may be perfectly happy writing about every single detail about that day, no matter how insignificant—and also be completely unaware that there are other ways he might tell his story. In a conference with this child, I might point out that he could, instead, choose to focus his piece on the most important moment of the day. If it were up to this child to initiate conferences, I probably wouldn't have an opportunity to help him see that there are other possibilities for structuring a story besides "bed to bed" until he was finished, when it might be too late to suggest such a major revision.

Occasionally, when I sat down next to students to initiate conferences, they asked me if I could confer with them later that period, or on a different day. Usually, they were in a writing "groove" and didn't want to be interrupted, so I honored their requests.

After several years of workshop teaching, I began to honor some student requests for my time. Since I wanted to help students become independent writers—and since I realized that part of what it meant to become independent was learning when to depend on other writers for feedback and assistance—I felt it was important to give students the opportunity to seek me out, too. Once the school year was under way and I felt that students understood what conferences were about, I invited them to request conferences. I told them they could approach me one-on-one after a mini-lesson or in between conferences and ask for a conference. (I also let them know they should never, ever interrupt me to ask for help while I was conferring with one of their classmates.) Students knew I would ask them if they had had a peer conference, if there was a strategy they had heard me talk about in a recent mini-lesson they could use, or if there was a text we had read as a class that they could look at to get some ideas to help them with their own writing. If they had already tried these strategies—and they hadn't worked—I usually agreed to see them sometime that period or the next day. During any given period, then, I initiated some conferences, and students the others.

Many teachers in the Reading and Writing Project community have developed their own strategies to strike a balance between conferences they initiate and conferences their students initiate. In Donna

Santman's sixth-grade classroom in I.S. 89 in Manhattan, she asks her students to drop her a note in a "Problem Basket" when they run into difficulties and want her help. In between conferences, Donna checks for notes and then often has conferences with these students. When Alexa Stott taught third grade at P.S. 199 in Manhattan, she wrote the names of three students she planned to see each period on the blackboard, and then left space for two more students to sign up for conferences with her.

How Much Time Should a Conference Take?

The most precious resource we have to give students is our time. In a typical forty-five-minute writing workshop period—which usually begins with a ten-minute mini-lesson and ends with a five-minute share session—we have thirty minutes of time to confer with students. How we choose to divide those thirty minutes is a decision that influences the quality of the conversations we have with students, and how often we can see them. It's important, then, for us to think hard about how many of these precious minutes we plan to give to each student in a conference.

We could use those thirty minutes to confer with as many students as possible. If we make this choice, we can see all of our students every two to three days, but our conversations with them will be rushed—and superficial. Or we could decide to concentrate on conferring with just one or two students. We would have a luxurious amount of time for each conference, but we would only see each student in the class every three to four weeks.

I try to see four or five students during each writing workshop period, which means that each conference is *on average* five minutes long. Five minutes is enough time to have a quality conversation with each student, and (in a class of thirty students) see each of them every six to eight days. If I'm able to make a teaching decision quickly, a conference might take only three or four minutes. Or if I need to give a student a lot of assistance during the have-a-go, then a conference might take seven or eight minutes. Rarely, however, are my conferences shorter than three minutes or longer than eight. I'm simply not willing to rush conversations with students, nor am I willing to see students less frequently.

When I've suggested to teachers that they try to see students every six to eight days, some have said, "That's it? How will each student get enough one-on-one attention to help them grow as writers?" In response, I've urged them to take a long-range view, and think about how many conferences each child will have with us across the school year. I've pointed out that if we're seeing students every six to eight days, that's twenty to thirty conferences per student in a school year. Those twenty to thirty conferences—in combination with daily mini-lessons and share sessions—give students the support they need to grow as writers. I've also pointed out those twenty to thirty conferences represent more one-on-one teaching than most of us received during all the years of our elementary and secondary educations combined.

DECISIONS, DECISIONS. WE make hundreds of decisions as we plan for the special events in our lives. Each of those decisions has an impact on these events in ways big and small. In the minutes right after Robin and I were married, my father-in-law, Harold Epstein, who originally had been skittish about our decision to be married on a mountain ridge, told us that he couldn't imagine feeling closer to God than he did that afternoon.

As we plan for conferences, we make decisions about where in the classroom we'll confer and which tools we'll bring with us and how much time we expect to give students in a typical conference. Each of these decisions affects the tone of the conversations we want to have with students, and ultimately how successful we may be in helping our students grow as writers.

References
Little, Jean. 1986. *Hey World, Here I Am.* New York: Harper.

"What Are All the *Other* Students Doing?" 7

Classroom Management in the Writing Workshop

During my first two years of workshop teaching, there were days when I found it nearly impossible to confer with students. A minute or two after I began a conference, the noise level in the room would become so loud that I couldn't hear the student I was conferring with. A quick glance around the room would reveal that most of my students were doing a great deal of talking but little writing. After each conference, I would settle the class down, only to have the decibels rise as soon as I began the next conference. Some days, I stopped conferring altogether and devoted all my energy to making sure students were writing. On those days I wanted to tear out my hair, and I wondered whether writing workshop was a workable idea after all.

As a staff developer, I've heard teachers new and experienced share similar stories of difficult days in their writing workshops—even difficult years. A few teachers have been so frustrated that they've burst into tears as they've recounted their difficulties.

For us to be able to confer, it's essential that the students with whom we *aren't* conferring are able to work independently for sustained periods of time. As we all know, fostering this kind of independence is a difficult—and critically important—classroom management challenge, especially when we're working with students who haven't been in writing workshops before. Unless our students can work independently, it can be almost impossible to conduct conferences.

The following management skills can help us make writing workshop a place where students can work independently while we confer with individual students:

- Envisioning the workshop.
- Teaching independence.
- Developing a repertoire of diagnostic questions.

In this chapter, I discuss these three management skills.

Envisioning the Workshop

It takes just a few minutes for visitors to Barbara Pinto's first-grade writing workshop at P.S. 6 in Manhattan or to Wanda Troy's third-/ fourth-grade workshop at P.S. 261 in Brooklyn to ask, "How does she do *this*?" By "this" they mean how the workshops of these teachers seem to run themselves. Students are sitting at tables, engrossed in their writing. Some of the students are talking to each other in quiet voices about their writing. A few students are out of their seats, getting supplies at the writing center or looking for a model text in the classroom library. And Barbara or Wanda is sitting at one of the tables, giving her full attention to the student with whom she is conferring.

Teachers like Barbara or Wanda who have well-managed writing workshops are great choreographers. They have a talent for envisioning exactly what they want students to be doing during the workshop. It's this envisionment work that makes it possible for us to confer with students without distraction. When our students know exactly what to do during the workshop, they will be able to work on their writing independently, and we will be able to give our full attention to conferring. In *Preventing Classroom Discipline Problems* (1994), Howard Seeman suggests that our success in envisioning the classroom environment will help us avoid disruptions:

> Environments push us into specific psychological sets; they tell us the range and kinds of behavior appropriate for where we are. The classroom environment can, in a way, tell students to care or not care about their behavior, or even suggest disruptive behavior. By "the classroom environment" we mean here more than just the *physical* environment, the room itself. We also mean: the seating arrangement of the class; the procedures of that room; your procedures; and the equipment used by you in the classroom. (123)

We begin our envisionment work by imagining how students will make the transition from the mini-lesson into writing time. When we effectively manage this transition, students have more time for writing, and we have more time for conferring. Managing the transition requires us to create predictable routines.

For example, if students gather in a meeting place for the mini-lesson, we need to develop a routine for moving students back to their seats—and we need to stick to it. Will we send students all back at once? Or by tables? Will students return to their seats one by one after we pass out their writing folders? Or will we ask students to raise their hands if they have a plan for their writing for that period, and as they raise their hands, send them back to their seats one by one?

If students remain at their seats for the mini-lesson, then we should give them a clear signal that the mini-lesson is over. This is their cue to begin writing. We might say something like, "Writers, it's time for you to get started with your work for today." Julia Suh, a teacher at M.S. 51 in Brooklyn, simply says, "Go," and her students get right to work.

As students settle into their writing, it helps if we circulate around the room. As we do so, we can nudge dawdlers to return to their seats. We can also stop by tables and remind students that it's time to get to work.

Students settle into their work more easily when their writing notebooks and drafts are already out on their desks or tables when the mini-lesson is over. Consequently, we might pass out writing folders or ask students to get their work out before they come to the meeting area.

We might designate the first five or ten minutes after the mini-lesson as a silent writing time. In Shoshana Jacob's first-grade class at P.S. 163 in Manhattan, for example, she called this, "No Talking, No Walking Time." With no talking or movement in the room during these few minutes, there were few distractions. Students could focus on rereading what they wrote the day before, making plans for that day's work, and getting started with their writing.

When we envision the workshop, we must decide what students will be doing during the workshop, and think about where and how students will do these things. At any given time during my writing workshops, students were doing one or more of the following activities:

- Working in their writers notebooks, either collecting ideas for future projects or developing seed ideas before starting drafts.
- Composing, revising, or editing drafts.
- Studying model pieces of literature.
- Having peer conferences.
- Getting writing supplies, literature, or references from the writing center.
- Getting a piece of writing ready for publication, perhaps by using a classroom computer or art supplies.

My students did most of their writing work at their seats. However, sometimes they needed to get up out of their seats and move to different locations in the classroom. They had peer conferences in the nooks and corners of the room. They visited the classroom library to find a text the class had been studying or the writing center to obtain a pair of scissors and tape for cutting and pasting their drafts. And, of course, they left the classroom to use the bathroom.

Since I didn't want this movement to distract students as they wrote—or me as I conferred—I needed to decide how students would move around the room. I *didn't* want to require them to get my permission to get out of their seats. It was distracting to me and the class when a student was waving her hand frantically, oohing and ahhing as she tried to get my attention while I was in the middle of a conference. It was also distracting when a student came up and tapped insistently on my shoulder when I was conferring.

Instead, I created simple systems that allowed my classroom to run itself so I could give my full attention to conferences. I decided that students could have a peer conference whenever they needed one, provided that one of the corners in the classroom designated for that purpose was empty. I decided that students could go to the writing center if there were no more than two students already there. And I allowed students to visit the bathroom as needed, if the bathroom pass was hanging on its hook by the door. Simple systems like these allowed the classroom to run itself, and it allowed me to give my full attention to conferences.

My students had a natural tendency to talk to each other as they wrote. I had to give this talk careful thought. In some of my workshops, I designated the tables where students wrote as quiet areas and the peer conference corners as talking places. In others, I allowed a low "buzz" at tables after the five- or ten-minute silent writing time. How loud a buzz I allowed depended on the classes I taught. Some classes seemed to work productively with a strong buzz, while others didn't. There was, of course, an upper limit to how much buzz I allowed. If the classroom was too noisy, I was unable to concentrate during conferences.

Once we've developed a clear image in our minds of what we want students to be doing during the workshop, we have to communicate this image to students. This communication is especially crucial during the early weeks of the school year.

During mini-lessons we talk about what students will do during the workshop. During the first few weeks of the school year in my own classroom, for example, I gave mini-lessons on how writers use their writers notebooks to collect and develop ideas, and on drafting, revising, and editing. I was defining for them what they could do during writing time. I put a chart on the wall with the title "What We Do During Writing Time." After a mini-lesson, I often added its subject to the list—"develop a seed idea in my notebook" or "work on revising my draft." A month or two into the school year, when I felt students had a sense of their options for writing time, I had them copy the chart into their writers notebook and then I took it down.

We might also devote early mini-lessons to peer conferences, and how students can initiate them, or the rules for visiting the writing center or bathroom. Don't worry that you are wasting valuable teaching time discussing subjects that don't directly address writing. The investment early in the year in spelling out for students how we want the classroom to work lays the foundation for students to become independent writers. And the more independent students become, the more time we'll be able to devote to teaching in conferences throughout the rest of the school year.

Learning More About Choreographing Writing Workshop
Several books describe with exceptional clarity the way their authors' writing workshops operated. Carol Avery's . . . *And With a Light Touch* (1993), Joanne Hindley's *In the Company of Children* (1996), Nancie Atwell's *In the Middle* (1998), and Randy Bomer's *Time for Meaning* (1995) are four such books that have helped thousands of teachers develop their vision of how to choreograph writing workshop.

It's also important to visit the classrooms of experienced writing workshop teachers. Seeing a workshop in action gives you a sense for its logic and rhythm that's hard to get from even the best books. If we're lucky, we can observe colleagues in our building. Some of us need to travel to other schools to learn from more experienced writing workshop teachers—schools in neighboring districts, even schools across the country.

Teaching Independence

I find it difficult to have conferences when there are six or seven children in a writing workshop who don't have an idea for a piece of writing and don't know how to find one, or when ten minutes into the workshop, half of the students are waving their hands and shouting, "I'm done." These students are still dependent on their teacher to help them move through the stages of the writing process. In these workshops, I can either rush from student to student to give them each a quick nudge, or have full-length conferences with a few of them while the class descends into chaos. Neither of these alternatives is acceptable.

Students *must* be able to work on their writing independently for a sustained period of time—a half hour or more—if we're going to be able to confer effectively. Since we want to start conferring as soon as we launch our workshops, teaching our students to be independent writers is a top priority during the early weeks of the school year, especially when we have students who are new to the writing workshop.

There are several basic things that student writers need to know how to do in order to write independently: they need to be able to find ideas; they need to be able to write fluently; and they need to know what to do once they've finished a piece. We must teach students how to do these things in mini-lessons and conferences.

It's quite common on the first day of writing workshop to hear many students say, "I don't know what to write about." Finding ideas for writing, then, is usually the focus of the first few mini-lessons. Within a couple of weeks, students develop a repertoire of strategies for finding ideas. This will probably include:

- Making a sketch.
- Looking around the room and letting the objects and people they see spark ideas.
- Getting ideas from rereading the pieces in their writing folders or entries in their writers notebook.
- Thinking back over the last several days of their lives.
- Free-writing.
- Thinking about something they have recently read, and then writing about what it made them think about.

We can also expect that some students will have limited fluency in the beginning of the school year. That is, they are unable to generate much writing about the topic they've chosen. We know that in kindergarten and first-grade classrooms, students will have trouble spelling unfamiliar words. During the first few days of a primary workshop, we often feel under siege by children asking, "How do you spell . . . ?" If our primary workshops are going to run smoothly, then we need to teach primary students the following strategies to help them grapple with writing words they do not know how to spell:

- Saying a word slowly ("stretching" it out) and listening for the sounds.
- Using an alphabet chart while stretching out a word.
- Using the "word wall" in the classroom.
- Asking a classmate how to spell the word.
- Taking their best shot at it and waiting to verify it later.

Those of us who teach in intermediate and upper grades have students who spend five minutes writing a couple of sentences and, unable to think of what else to say, then complain, "I'm stuck." And we have students who write "The End" on the bottom of the page, not because they've really come to the end of their pieces, but because they can't think of anything else to say. We need to teach these students strategies for getting unstuck and saying more about their topics:

- Rereading what they've written so far to jumpstart their thinking.
- Free-writing about the topic.
- Sketching what they're writing about.
- Reading what they've written to a classmate and having that classmate ask them questions.

Students also need to know what to do when they are genuinely finished with a draft. Early in the year, we need to teach them the procedures to follow once they're done. When primary students are finished, for example, they might write their name and stamp the date on the top of the page, read the piece to a classmate, and then put it in the side of their writing folder designated for finished pieces. In upper-grade classrooms, we might require children to have content conferences with peers, read over their pieces for spelling, punctuation, and grammar, and then make a final copy for publication. As the year progresses and we launch our primary and upper-grade classes into studies of revision and editing, we will expect students to do considerable revision and editing work before they go to publication.

Even after students are able to find ideas independently, generate lots of text, and revise and edit drafts, they are going to run into other difficulties. Some will get frustrated because they can't think of how to begin or end their pieces, or because they want to get the characters in their stories talking but they aren't sure how to write dialogue, or because they can't decide how to structure their pieces. And so on.

Students who are having these kinds of difficulties will want to confer with us. Since we won't always be available—and since it's unacceptable that they stop writing until they can have a conference with us—we have to teach them there are other places they can go for assistance:

- They can look at a piece of writing by an author they admire and see how she handled the problem they're facing.
- They can ask a classmate for help in a peer conference.
- They can bring their problem to their response group.

It isn't enough, of course, to tell students they can get help in these places. We have to teach students how to look at published writing and learn from it, and how to have effective peer conferences or response groups. These are all subjects we need to discuss in mini-lessons during the first few months of school.

Developing a Repertoire of Diagnostic Questions

Rarely will our workshops run without a hitch even after students learn how we want the workshop to operate and they become independent writers. As a teacher, I had to deal with some management issues almost every day. The buzz in the room became too loud. There were too many students—and, consequently, too much commotion—at the writing center. When such things happened, I was distracted and unable to give my full attention to conferences.

I handled these kinds of problems immediately. To quiet the buzz, I stopped the class and reminded students that writers—and their teacher—have trouble concentrating when there is too much noise in a room. Or I walked over to the writing center and sent students back to their seats. With the situation improved, I was able again to devote my full attention to conferring.

When a problem was persistent—for example, when I had to quiet the buzz in the room several times a period for several consecutive days—I raised the issue with the whole class. Sometimes, after a mini-lesson, I called the class's attention to the problem and restated the procedure or rule that had broken down. Other times, if the problem was particularly vexing, I canceled my mini-lesson and instead asked students for input in solving the problem.

However, there were times when it seemed that everything broke down at once. It wasn't just that children were talking loudly to each other at their tables, or wandering aimlessly about the classroom, or fighting over the bathroom pass every time a child returned with it. *All* of these things were happening simultaneously, all period long, sometimes for several days in a row, even weeks. Because students weren't doing much writing, I sometimes gave up on conferring altogether. Instead, I rushed from table to table and implored students to be quiet, led children by their arms back to their seats, and even stood in front of the blackboard, chalk in hand, putting checks next to the names of students who disrupted the class.

Over time, I learned that one or more of the following problems could be the cause of these serious breakdowns.

Are Students Invested in Their Writing?

Nothing is more important to ensuring that the workshop runs smoothly than students who are invested in their writing. When we have a critical mass of students in a class who don't feel invested, it can be extremely difficult to manage that class. Students who don't feel that writing is a good use of their time are more likely to talk and act out than those who do, no matter whether we start writing time with ten minutes of silence or insist repeatedly that they keep their voices down.

When we sense that students aren't invested in their writing, we have to figure out why they feel that way. In some classrooms, for example, I've noticed that students publish their writing only once, maybe twice, a year. When students aren't writing toward publication, their energy for writing quickly dissipates.

One way to ratchet up the energy in a workshop is to publish more frequently. My colleagues and I at the Reading and Writing Project suggest that primary students publish on average once every two weeks and upper-grade students once a month.

By "publishing," I simply mean that students share finished drafts with an audience. In the primary grades, the audience might simply be a student's writing partner. It might be the children who are sitting together at a table, who read their finished pieces to each other. Or the audience might be the whole class gathered together around the authors chair to hear classmates read pieces aloud.

Many upper-grade teachers post publication dates on their bulletin boards weeks or months in advance so that students can write with publishing in mind. In many New York City classrooms, when the publication date arrives, students place their finished pieces on their tables, along with a blank sheet of paper for comments. Students spend an hour circulating around the classroom, reading their classmates' writing and jotting down responses. At P.S. 321 in Brooklyn, students in every class share their writing with not only their classmates, but their relatives, too. Teachers reserve the school lobby for class writing celebrations, and then invite parents and grandparents to come hear students give readings of their pieces.

Another reason students may not be invested in their writing is because they don't believe it is a meaningful activity. When students feel there's no payoff involved, they go to great lengths to avoid it. Writing, after all, is very hard work. I don't know anyone who wants to work hard at something that feels meaningless.

I've never taught a class that didn't include a few students who didn't see any point in writing. In fact, in some classes full of students who had never been in a writing workshop before, most students felt that way at the beginning of the school year. It takes time—weeks or even months if students have had negative experiences with writing—to help students discover that writing can be worthwhile.

It's critically important that we put these disaffected students in the company of writers. The best place to start is by reading aloud pieces written by published authors. When they are moved by literature, students begin to understand that they, too, can have the same impact on readers.

We shouldn't underestimate the power of sharing our own writing with students. When I was a classroom teacher, I took my seventh graders step by step through the process of writing a memoir about my seventh-grade girlfriend. I showed them everything from entries in my writers notebooks to edited drafts. Not only did my students get lots of ideas for strategies and techniques they could try in their writing, they also saw that I had written honestly about an important experience in my life. And it didn't hurt that they heard their classmates respond with raucous laughter and nods of understanding. By living my life as a writer in front of students, I helped many of them see that writing can be meaningful and worth spending time on. I'm not saying all teachers have to write up the most vulnerable moments of their childhood or adolescence and share them with their students. But it is helpful if teachers have written something their students can relate to; a memoir about a favorite pet or relative would do just fine.

We also need to read aloud writing written by students who are excited about writing. When we read a piece written by a student that wows his peers, we open their eyes to their own potential as authors. They come to realize they too can move other people with their written words.

Do Students Make Plans and Set Goals for Their Writing?

When writers come to their writing each day with a sense of purpose, they're much less likely to get off track or be distracted. We need to teach students to be the kind of writers who begin writing time by making plans for *what* they're going to do that period. Are they going to spend the period working on their leads? Making revisions? Or checking spelling? And we need to teach students to be the kind of writers who set goals for *how much* they're going to accomplish each period. How much text will they try to write? Which sections of their pieces will they revise?

To teach students to make writing plans and set writing goals, we first have to give them reason for doing so. In the previous section, I made a case for setting frequent publication dates. Not only do these dates invite student investment in their writing, they also make it necessary for students to become the kind of writers who make plans and set goals. Students have to learn to figure out what kind of writing work they need to do each day, and how much of it, if they're going to have pieces ready on time.

In addition to setting publication dates, we can also set deadlines for completing first drafts, for completing revisions, and for finishing edits. These deadlines help students think about the next few days, a manageable chunk of time. Or we can encourage students to set their own deadlines, and stick to them.

We also need to teach students how to make plans and set goals. At the end of mini-lessons, before students start working on their writing, we can encourage students to get in the habit of making plans and setting goals for the period by using one of the following strategies:

- Ask students to turn to a classmate and tell what they'll be doing that period, and how much they plan to write.
- Have students jot down on a Post-it what their writing plans and goals are for the period, which they stick at the top of the draft they're working on.
- Have students jot down their plans and goals in an "assignment box" in their writers notebooks.
- Ask each student in turn to say aloud what their plans and goals are for the period. Nancie Atwell (1998) calls this strategy the "status-of-the-class conference" (140).
- Have students "write to the X"—that is, they write an "X" on the line in their writers notebook or draft where they hope to be by the end of that day's workshop

We can also have students use these same strategies at the end of the workshop to help them make plans for what they will be working on that night or the next day.

It's important that students know we have high expectations. At the beginning of conferences, we can ask if students are carrying through with the plans they made earlier in the period, or check to see if they're on track to realize their goals. Writing partnerships can also hold students accountable. At the end of each day's workshop, writing partners can ask each other if they got done what they thought they would, or wrote as much as they had intended.

We can't be afraid to establish consequences for students who consistently fail to realize their plans or goals. We might, for example, keep them in from recess or after school to work on their writing, or require them to complete their writing at home. Consequences like these are not punitive; they help hold students accountable and make it more likely they will start sticking to the plans and goals they set.

Am I a Gatekeeper?

If we take on the role of "gatekeeper," our workshops will probably break down. We are gatekeepers when we don't allow students to move to the next step in the writing process without first conferring with us and getting our okay. For example, when we insist that students have a revision conference with us before they can edit, we are being gatekeepers. When we are gatekeepers, our focus is usually on making students' writing better, not on helping them become better writers.

The problem is that only one student can pass through the gate at a time. At any given time in our workshops, however, there might be several students who are making their final revisions to a draft. If we required all of them to have a revision conference with us before they could edit, then all of them except the one with whom we're conferring would be waiting their turn for a conference, with nothing to do but wait. It shouldn't surprise us if some of these students begin to fool around and disrupt the class.

Instead of gatekeeping, we need to allow students to move from one stage of the writing process to another when *they* decide they're ready. And we need to become comfortable with conferring with students wherever they are in the process of writing their pieces, not just when they're revising. To help students become better writers, we need to help them get better at all aspects of writing.

Is My Presence Felt Around the Room?

Let's face it: kids are kids. If we don't make our presence felt around the classroom, some of them will talk and fool around instead of working on their writing.

We could react to this by assuming the persona of police officers. But if we're always patrolling the classroom, we won't be able to confer with them. Thankfully, there are steps short of becoming cops that we can take to make our presence felt in every corner of the room.

First, it's important that we confer where students write, at their tables or desks. Students can't help but feel our presence when we spend the period amongst them, instead of behind our desk or at a special conference table (which can make some students on the other side of the room feel they can get away with not writing).

In between conferences, I take a minute to walk the room. During this time, I put my hand on the shoulders of students who seem to be losing their focus and say a few words to get them back on track.

Do Students Have Easy Access to Writing Materials?
Writers have many good reasons for getting up out of their seats (and not just to pace up and down in the room until ideas pop into their heads). Stumped about how to end a chapter, I get up to find my copy of Ralph Fletcher's *What a Writer Needs* to reread his chapter endings. Unsure of how to spell a word, I go look for it in a dictionary on the bookshelf. If my laptop battery gets dangerously low in power, I rush to find the power cord and plug it in before the machine shuts itself off. And so forth. During most writing sessions, though I spend most of the time writing, I'm usually out of my seat a few times.

Student writers are no different. They will invariably need paper and scissors and the stapler. They will want a copy of the text we read them in a mini-lesson to study its lead. Or they will want correction fluid to fix a mistake on a final draft.

We want our students to have easy access to materials they need—and to know they may go get them as needed—or else our workshops will break down. When students are unable to get materials, then they become dependent on us to supply them with what they need. We don't want this responsibility. It's hard to concentrate on conferences when students are frantically waving their hands and calling out that they need a pencil or a piece of paper. And the time that we spend getting paper for students or locating a text that we used in a mini-lesson the previous week is time that we could be using to confer.

We need to designate special places in the classroom for writing materials. Many teachers, for example, have writing centers where students can get paper and other supplies, and use the stapler. Many teachers have a special section in their classroom libraries for texts the whole class has studied in mini-lessons.

WHEN I WAS a classroom teacher, there were times when my students seemed unable to work independently in my writing workshops. Consequently, I found it difficult to give individual students my undivided attention in conferences.

We all have had these days, and will inevitably have them again. When they happen, we need to step back and ask ourselves, "What's going on here?" We may figure out that we need to help students better understand how we want the workshop to operate. Or we may need to teach students strategies to help them be independent writers. Or we may realize there is a problem such as little student investment in writing or a failure to project our presence around the classroom, and we need to take immediate steps to address it.

References
Atwell, Nancie. 1998. *In the Middle.* Portsmouth, NH: Heinemann.

Avery, Carol. 1993. *. . . And With a Light Touch.* Portsmouth, NH: Heinemann.

Bomer, Randy. 1995. *Time for Meaning.* Portsmouth, NH: Heinemann.

Hindley, Joanne. 1996. *In the Company of Children.* York, ME: Stenhouse.

Seeman, Howard. 1994. *Preventing Classroom Discipline Problems.* Lancaster, PA: Technomic Publishing.

Afterword

Getting Back to Conferring Basics

Right after I finished writing the chapters of this book, I became obsessed with, of all things, the music of the Beatles. For a whole week, instead of sitting with my writers notebook at the kitchen table and trying to figure out how I wanted to end the book, I lay on the rug of the living room, listening to Beatles CDs play on the stereo.

As it turned out, listening to the Beatles was a great writing strategy for me. Listening to their music—in combination with a chance encounter with someone from my teaching past—helped remind me of the one final piece of advice about writing conferences I have to share in the book. A piece of advice, in fact, that is as important as anything else I have written so far.

I didn't become obsessed with just any Beatles music, but the songs they first rehearsed in January 1969, in preparation for their first live concert in three years. In the time since they had stopped touring, John Lennon, Paul McCartney, George Harrison, and Ringo Starr had taken rock 'n' roll music to a new place, but the songs they had created in the studio were so complex they couldn't be performed by the group on stage. In January 1969, the Beatles wanted to get back to their roots as performing musicians and write music that the four of them could once again sing together to an audience.

As I lay on the floor of my apartment, I listened over and over again to "Don't Let Me Down," which John Lennon had written for his new love, Yoko Ono. The song is a return to basics. Just like during the old days, it required just three guitars and a drumset for the band to play the song. And unlike the lyrics of many of the songs John had written in the past few years, songs like "Strawberry Fields Forever," the lyrics to "Don't Let Me Down" are clear and direct. Of all the songs the Beatles wrote, this one—a song about falling in love for the first time—is one of my all-time favorites. As I listened to "Don't Let Me Down" over and over again, I thought about how fitting it was that this band, which had burst onto the music scene singing of holding hands, would get back to their roots five years later by singing of being in love for the first time.

In my thirty-eight years, I've learned that my obsessions usually have something to do with the issues present in my life at the time I have them. Finishing my book certainly qualified as an issue. But I hadn't yet connected my obsession with the Beatles to writing the ending. I hadn't yet realized that I needed to end my book by getting back to conferring basics. At this point in the story, all I thought I was doing was enjoying good music.

Then I ran into Aurora. I had driven into Manhattan (with the Beatles cranked up loudly on the car stereo) to pick up my wife, Robin, at work. When I stepped into the door of Robin's workplace, a young woman said, "Mr. Anderson." The young woman was a security guard. That she knew my name didn't surprise me. Robin had called down to the security desk to let her know I would be arriving.

"Mr. Anderson," she said again. I looked at the young woman more closely. She was in her early twenties. There was something vaguely familiar about her.

"Mr. Anderson," she said, this time exasperated. "Don't you remember me? You were my sixth-grade teacher."

"Aurora?" I said. "Aurora . . . Oh my gosh, it's you!" I was stunned. Aurora was one of my favorite students in the sixth-grade class I taught in the Bronx eleven years ago, the first year I ever launched a writing workshop. Here she was, all grown up, taller than me.

Aurora and I told stories about some of the things that happened that year, and we laughed over and over again. She told me she was almost finished college and was thinking about becoming a lawyer or a U.S. Marshal. Finally, I turned to go upstairs. Just before leaving, though, I said wistfully, "I've learned so much about teaching writing—I even have a book on teaching writing coming out soon—and I really wish I could teach you and the rest of Class 6-11 again today somehow." For a long moment, Aurora looked at me, surprised by what I said. Then she said, "You taught me how to write, Mr. Anderson, and believe me, that was the last thing on my mind when I started in your class. I've had a lot of teachers who didn't give a crap about me, but you did."

The following week, when I finally sat down with my writers notebook to sketch out the ending for the book, I found myself thinking not about conferring, but about running into Aurora. I began to get annoyed with myself. First the Beatles, now Aurora. What the heck was wrong with me? I couldn't remember that much about my first writing conferences eleven years ago, except that they didn't go well initially—and I had already written about that in Chapter 3. Again and again, however, I found myself thinking not about the Afterword, but about running into Aurora.

Finally, I gave in and decided to write in my writers notebook about Aurora and her class and my first writing workshop—although I couldn't imagine what smart thinking about conferring I could possibly squeeze out of my memories of my first writing conferences. As a writer, however, I've learned to trust the things that distract me as I write, the things that tug me away from what I think I *want* to write. These things usually pull me toward thinking about what I *need* to write. I wondered what I would find out.

To help me get started, I went downstairs to the basement of my apartment building, where I knew I had stored mementos of the years I spent as a classroom teacher. As I searched my filing cabinet for the right drawer, I was struck that over the years I've collected only a few kinds of things: artifacts from my family, notes and letters from junior and high school girlfriends, mementos from the time my wife and I were dating—and thick files of my students' writing. Hmmm, I thought, that's something to write about right there.

After finding the files, I carried them upstairs. As I walked through the basement hall and rode up the elevator, I realized I already knew what I would find in the files. Aurora's memoir of her cat, Skye. Tunde's detective stories. Wendy's piece about the witch who lived next door to her grandmother in the Dominican Republic. Dawana's memoir of her up-and-down relationship with her best friend, Nicole. Although my students had written these pieces eleven years ago, and today they're all as grown up as Aurora, I could still remember what they had written about, even what their handwriting looked like. I could even remember some of the comments I had written on top of their papers.

Opening the files, I also found a copy of *Wow! Magazine,* the anthology of student writing that I had typed page by page on a manual typewriter at the end of that year. As I read each piece, I could see each student clear as day in my mind, hear their voices, see them tapping their pencils or the faraway look they got when they wrote.

When I got to Veronica's piece about her sister, Erika, I read it over and over again, remembering. I remembered that on the day that I launched writing workshop that year, it was Veronica who set the tone for the year that followed. In my mini-lesson, I had told my students a few stories from my life as examples of the kinds of things that they could write about. Then I asked if anyone wanted to tell some of their own stories. There was a long awkward pause. Then Veronica, a short, quiet girl, stood up. "I'm going to write about my sister, Erika. She died last year of leukemia. She was my older sister, and I still need her, but she's not there for me anymore. I miss her so much."

Veronica's piece about her sister reminded me of how the power and deep emotion of her spoken words on that first day of writing workshop transformed my class. A community of students who wrote honestly about what mattered to them in their lives was born in that moment.

Rereading Veronica's piece, I realized that the power and deep emotion of her words on that first day of writing workshop had transformed me, too. By sharing her life, Veronica became a different girl in my eyes. No longer was she just the girl who sat in the first seat in the fifth row. No longer was she just the girl who usually got her homework in on time. Now she was Veronica, who had lost her older sister. Now she was Veronica, the girl who had the courage to speak honestly of her terrible loss. Now she was Veronica, the girl who needed to write to make sense of her life. For the first time in my career—this was my second year in the classroom— I had been affected by a student's life. I would never be the same teacher again.

After reading my students' writing, I wrote in my notebook. I wrote about how smitten I was with my students that year, and how I talked about them and their writing incessantly. I remembered how I read Elaine's memoir about her impish sister, Denise, to my colleagues. And how I read Julio's story about breaking up with his girlfriend, Lizzy, to my roommate. And how I called my mother and read her Ebony's piece about the boy who was shot dead in front of her on the elevator of her apartment building.

And when the year ended, I remembered, I begged my students to let me keep some of their precious stories. I didn't want to let go of this class, but by holding on to some of their words, I wouldn't have to let go completely. I could keep part of them forever.

Aurora took me back to the day I launched my first writing workshop, back to the day I learned one of the most basic things about teaching writing. To teach writing well—to confer with student writers well—we must be affected by our students and the details of their lives. That is, we need to fall in love with our students for the first time.

As I thought about this lesson, I thought about the students whom I have featured in this book. I think each conference with them is a good one. As I thought about Doran and Becky and William and Kamara, I reflected that an important reason these conferences had gone well was because I had been affected by the details of each of their lives. I had fallen in love with each of them.

Take Natalie, the second grader I conferred with in Chapter 4. I want to share the moment that the details of this child's life moved me. And then I want to talk about how being affected by Natalie's life helped me have a good conference with her.

Natalie's class was studying how writers turn the entries they have written about their seed ideas in their writers notebooks into drafts. When I suggested to Natalie's teacher, Nicole Harris, that in that day's mini-lesson we have a student read her entries aloud and have her classmates give her advice about what kind of writing she could make out of those entries, Ms. Harris suggested Natalie. I was pleased that Ms. Harris picked Natalie because when I had read my writing to the class during previous mini-lessons, I had noticed that Natalie smiled and laughed in all the right places. When it was time for her to read, Natalie sat in the big chair in front of her class, flipped nervously through the pages of her notebook, then began to read the entries she had written about her dad, about how they had sock fights and climbed rocks in Central Park and played soccer.

I listened intently as Natalie read those entries about her father. On one level, I was trying to imagine Natalie's entries as a picture book or a collection of poems, or as some other kind of writing. On another, deeper, level, however, I was listening as the father of Anzia, who was then eighteen months old and is one of the two great loves of my life. As I listened to Natalie read, I couldn't help but be affected by her words, by her life, by the details of the relationship she had with her dad. Anzia isn't yet as articulate or literate as Natalie, but when she shouts, "Daddy!" when I walk in the door of my apartment, or when she says, "Daddy . . . help!" at the playground when she wants to climb to the top of the slide, she's seeing me in the same way Natalie sees her dad. As I listened to Natalie read her entries, I began to see her not just as one of the students in Ms. Harris's class, but as another father's daughter, a daughter loved by her father as much as I love my own. The particulars of Natalie's life affected me.

In the conference I had with Natalie later that period, I made the conversational moves and did the intellectual work I have discussed in this book. But that isn't the only reason why the conference went well. You see, once I've been affected by students, I *want* to confer with them. I *want* to find out how they are doing the work of fashioning those precious lives and interests into pieces of writing. I *want* to teach them something about writing well in order to help them affect their readers now and in the future in the same way that I've been affected. Falling in love with students motivates me to fulfill my role and responsibilities as well as I can in conferences with them.

Aurora took me back to another lesson about conferring well I learned earlier in my career, and it's this: students need to fall in love with us, too. They, too, need to be affected by the details of our lives. Conferences go well when students come to see us as people with whom they genuinely want to talk.

Students will only become affected by the details of our lives if we are willing to share them with them. We share by telling them stories and by reading them our writing. In another one of the files I brought up from the basement soon after I ran into Aurora, I found a piece of writing I wrote and read to the eighth graders I taught in Kentucky two years after I taught Aurora's class. During a genre study of memoir, I wrote my own memoir about my first love, Cathy, the girl I went out with in seventh grade. Here's part of that memoir:

> [After our first date], my mother picked us up at the bowling alley. She brought our toy poodle along for the ride. When we arrived at Cathy's house, her parents invited us all in. I carried the poodle in my arms.
>
> After listening to our parents talking politely in the living room for several minutes, Cathy beckoned for me to follow her to her room. After I entered, Cathy shut and locked the door.
>
> There I stood in the center of her room, still holding the poodle in my arms. Cathy sat down on the edge of her bed.
>
> "Why don't you sit down?" she suggested.
>
> "No, thanks," I replied. The poodle was nervous, and I was afraid she would wet the carpet. So Cathy sat, and I con-

tinued to stand in the middle of the room, and we continued to carry on our first date conversation.

Not until later, after we had broken up, did I realize that I had chosen a toy poodle over a first kiss. I guess I made the choice out of the fear of having my arms around any creature other than a small dog, especially the strange and mysterious creature known as a girl.

As I reread this piece, I remembered I had once heard Don Graves say that to teach writing well, we should know at least five details about the lives and interests of each child we teach. I believe that every student in our classes should know at least five details about our lives and interests, and probably many more. Sharing these details makes us real, real in a way that helps students see us not just as teachers, but as people.

When students see us as people, they are more likely to want to talk with us about their writing. Think about it. If an acquaintance asks you, "How's it going?" you probably won't give a detailed—and honest—answer about what's going on with you unless you really know and care about and trust the person who's asking. And when students see us not only as people, but as people who write about their lives, they know we have something in common to talk about—the work we do to make pieces of writing about our experiences.

As a former teacher of seventh and eighth graders, I know what a vulnerable feeling it can be to share our lives with students. Jasmine, for example, was one of the eighth graders I taught in Kentucky. In the file of things I kept from the year I taught her, the file that contained the memoir I wrote about my seventh-grade girlfriend, there was also this piece that Jasmine had written, a piece that managed to parody both my interests *and* my writing workshop:

The Proven Usefulness of the Writing Process
by Jasmine Rizer

"Paul, you bloody fool," said John Lennon. He was standing in his living room holding the original copy of "Yesterday." "We've got to take this song through the writing process."

Paul McCartney stared at him blankly. "That's fine, John, but what's the writin' process?"

"It's very important, that's all," replied John, sitting down cross-legged on the floor in front of his living room table. He glanced up at McCartney. "Did you pre-write, Paul?" Paul shook his head. Lennon glowered.

"It would be so much better if you had pre-written," he remarked . . . "[And] I still think we could work on that lead a bit. It's such a typical lead . . . 'Yesterday, all my troubles seemed so far away, now it looks as though they're here to stay . . .' Maybe you could open with some dialogue instead . . ."

"Oh, no."

Throughout the years I taught middle school students, they needled me about the stories I told them. That was a small price to pay for how comfortable most of them seemed in writing conferences with me. And, by the way, nine years after she wrote "The Proven Usefulness of the Writing Process," I still hear from Jasmine. She asks me now and then if I still love the Beatles.

When we've allowed ourselves to be affected by the stuff of our students' lives and they've been affected by ours—and we have a clear sense of our role in a conference—it's a powerful combination. Our conferences are more likely to go well when we have all come to see each other not just as teachers and students, but as real people, too.

I want to end by telling the story of the concert the Beatles finally did have in late January, 1969.

It was lunchtime on a blustery, cold late January day in 1969 when the band walked onto the roof of their London office to play what would be their last concert. For the next half hour, John, Paul, George, and Ringo played the songs they had spent the last few weeks bringing through the writing process—"Don't Let Me Down" among them. Hundreds of surprised people gathered in the streets below to listen. When the London police arrived and threatened to arrest the group for creating a public nuisance, the concert ended.

Right after the Beatles played the final chord of their last song, "Get Back," John Lennon said, "I'd like to say thank you on behalf of the group and ourselves and I hope we passed the audition." Four weeks earlier, the Beatles had come together to try to get back to the basics of being a performing group again. During the thirty minutes they played together on the roof, they got back. They felt like they had in the old days, the days before they became world-famous, the days they were just another unknown band hoping to pass an audition and get a record contract.

In this book, I've presented a lot of ideas about conferring. I've talked about seeing the writing conference as a conversation. I've talked about our role as teachers in the conversation, and our students' roles, too. I've talked about teaching our students to have writing mentors, about mini-lessons, and about class management.

There's a lot to think about in a writing conference. As we get better at conferring, though, it's essential that we remember the most important lessons about having good writing conferences. To confer well, we need to be affected by students, and them by us. We need to be in love for the first time.

Appendix

Mentor Texts

The following texts are ones my colleagues at the Reading and Writing Project and I make sure we tuck into our carry bags each morning before we visit schools because we know we'll be sure to talk about them with students in conferences that day. I have categorized the texts by the grade levels in which we typically use them—intermediate and upper-grade or primary—and by genre.

While it was tempting to describe the ways we use each text in conferences, I decided against it. I felt it was more important that you fall in love with these texts yourself, and find your own reasons for weaving them into conferences. Chances are, you'll find ways for using the texts that my colleagues and I haven't considered.

Mentor Texts for Writers in Intermediate and Upper Grades
Memoir
Excerpts from the following books:
> *Boy* by Roald Dahl (Penguin).
> *Childtimes* by Eloise Greenfield and Lessie Little Jones (Crowell).
> *A Girl from Yamhill* by Beverly Cleary (Dell).
> *Hey World, Here I Am* by Jean Little (Harper).
> *House on Mango Street* by Sandra Cisneros (Vintage).
> *Little By Little* by Jean Little (Viking).
> *Looking Back: A Book of Memories* by Lois Lowry (Houghton Mifflin).
> *Oddballs* by William Sleator (Dutton).

Poetry

The Dreamkeeper and Other Poems by Langston Hughes (A. Knopf).

Going Over to Your Place by Paul Janeczko (Bradbury).

Honey I Love, and Other Love Poems by Eloise Greenfield (Harper).

I Feel a Little Jumpy Around You by Naomi Shihab Nye and Paul B. Janeczko (Simon & Schuster).

Poetspeak by Paul Janeczko (Bradbury).

Pteradactlys and Pizza edited by Lee Bennett Hopkins (Trumpet).

Sky Scrape, City Scrape: Poems of City Life by Jane Yolen (Woodbury/Boyds Mill).

Spectacular Science: A Book of Poems edited by Lee Bennett Hopkins (Simon & Schuster).

Sweetcorn by James Stevenson (Greenwillow).

This Same Sky poems selected by Naomi Shihab Nye (Four Winds).

Picture Books

Aunt Flossie's Hats (and Crabcakes Later) by Elizabeth Howard (Clarion).

Bigmama's by Donald Crews (Greenwillow).

Come On, Rain! by Karen Hesse (Scholastic).

Fireflies by Julie Brinkloe (Aladdin).

Grandfather's Journey by Allen Say (Houghton Mifflin).

Jamaica Louise James by Amy Hest (Candlewick).

My Mama Had A Dancing Heart by Libba Moore Gray (Orchard).

Night in the Country by Cynthia Rylant (Bradbury).

No Mirrors In My Nana's House by Ysaye M. Barnwell (Harcourt Brace).

Owl Moon by Jane Yolen (Scholastic).

The Pain and the Great One by Judy Blume (Dell).

The Relatives Came by Cynthia Rylant (Bradbury).

Salt Hands by Jane Aragon (Dutton).

Scarecrow by Cynthia Rylant (Harcourt Brace).

Shortcut by Donald Crews (Greenwillow).

So Much by Trish Cooke (Candlewick).

Tar Beach by Faith Ringgold (Crown).

We Had a Picnic This Sunday Past by Jacqueline Woodson (Hyperion).

What You Know First by Patricia MacLachlan (HarperCollins).

When I Was Young in the Mountains by Cynthia Rylant (Dutton).

Short Fiction

> *Baseball in April* collection of stories by Gary Soto (Harcourt Brace).
>
> Collections edited by Donald Gallo, especially *Sixteen* and *Visions* (Delacorte).
>
> "Eleven" by Sandra Cisneros in *Woman Hollering Creek and Other Stories* (Vintage).
>
> *Every Living Thing* collection of stories by Cynthia Rylant (Bradbury).
>
> *Short Takes* collection of stories by Elizabeth Segal (Lothrop, Lee & Shepard).
>
> Stories that appear in *Cricket* magazine.

Novels

Excerpts from the following books:

> *The Cookcamp* by Gary Paulsen (Yearling).
>
> *Fig Pudding* by Ralph Fletcher (Clarion).
>
> *From the Notebooks of Melanin Sun* by Jacqueline Woodson (Scholastic).
>
> *Toning the Sweep* by Angela Johnson (Orchard).

Nonfiction

I've found editorials and feature articles mainly in newspapers and magazines. In every city I've lived, I've found excellent editorials on the op-ed pages of that city's newspapers. While I've found some feature articles in those newspapers, too—especially in the children's sections of those papers—I've had more success in finding articles in the magazines students read, such as *Boys Life, Cobblestone, Faces, Harvey, National Geographic World, New Moon,* and *Ranger Rick*.

Mentor Texts for Writers in Primary Grades
Memoir/Story

> *Bigmama's* by Donald Crews (Greenwillow).
>
> *The Chalk Doll* by Charollote Pomerantz (Lippincott).
>
> Excerpts from *Babybug* and *Ladybug* magazines.
>
> *Flower Garden* by Eve Bunting (Harcourt Brace).
>
> *Hairs = Pelitos* by Sandra Cisneros (A. Knopf).
>
> The Jump at the Sun board books by Dessie and Chevelle Moore, such as *Good Morning* or *Getting Dressed* (HarperFestival).

The Leaving Morning and *One of Three* by Angela Johnson (Orchard).
The Moon Was the Best by Charlotte Zolotow (Greenwillow).
"More, More, More" Said the Baby by Vera B. Williams (Greenwillow).
One Afternoon by Umi Heo (Orchard Books).
One Hot Summer Day by Nina Crews (Greenwillow).
The Relatives Came by Cynthia Rylant (Bradbury).
Shortcut by Donald Crews (Greenwillow).
When I Was Five by Arthur Howard (Harcourt Brace).
When I Was Little by Jamie Lee Curtis (HarperCollins).
When I Was Young in the Mountains by Cynthia Rylant (Dutton).

Poetry

All the Small Poems and Fourteen More by Valerie Worth (Farrar, Straus, and Giroux).
Honey I Love by Eloise Greenfield (Harper).
Street Music: City Poems by Arnold Adoff (HarperCollins).
Sweetcorn by James Stevenson (Greenwillow).

Nonfiction

All About Rattlesnakes by Jim Arnosky (Scholastic).
Cynthia Rylant's Everyday books such as *Everyday House* and *Everyday Pets* (Bradbury).
From Tadpole to Frog by Wendy Pfeffer, and other books in the HarperCollins Let's-Read-And-Find-Out Science series.
Katja's Book of Mushrooms by Katya Arnold and Sam Swope (Holt).
The Very Hungry Caterpillar by Eric Carle (Philomel).
What's What: A Guessing Game by Mary Serfozo (Margaret K. McElderry Books).

Concept Books

A to Z Look and See by Audean Johnson (Random House).
City Seen from A to Z by Rachel Isadora (Greenwillow).
10 Black Dots by Donald Crews (Greenwillow).
Ten, Nine, Eight by Molly Bang (Tupelo).

List Books

Hello, Lulu by Caroline Uff (Walker & Co.).
It Looked Like Spilt Milk by Charles Shaw (Harper Trophy).

Just Like Daddy by Frank Ash (Simon Schuster).
My Dad Is Awesome by Nick Butterworth (Candlewick).
My Dog by Heidi Goennel (Orchard).

Label Books
  Night At the Fair by Donald Crews (Greenwillow).
  Parade by Donald Crews (Greenwillow).

Index